SILENT SISTERS

SERIES IN HEALTH CARE FOR WOMEN
Series Editor: **Phyllis Noerager Stern,** DNS, RN, FAAN

Helpers in Childbirth: Midwifery Today   Oakley and Houd
Menstruation, Health and Illness   Taylor and Woods
Silent Sisters: A Study of Homeless Women   Russell

In Preparation

*Violence Against Women: Nursing, Research, Education,
   and Practice Issues*   Sampselle

SILENT SISTERS
A Study of Homeless Women

Betty G. Russell, Ph.D.
Baltimore, Maryland

⬤HEMISPHERE PUBLISHING CORPORATION
A member of the Taylor & Francis Group
New York   Washington   Philadelphia   London

SILENT SISTERS: A Study of Homeless Women

1 2 3 4 5 6 7 8 9 0   B R B R   9 8 7 6 5 4 3 2 1

This book was set in Times Roman by Hemisphere Publishing Corporation. The editor was Amy Lyles Wilson; the production supervisor was Peggy M. Rote; and the typesetters were Darrell D. Larsen, Jr. and Wayne Hutchins. Cover design by Debra Eubanks Riffe.

Cover art and inside art by Frank Russell. Copyright © 1991 by Frank Russell.

Printing and binding by Braun-Brumfield, Inc.

A CIP catalog record for this book is available from the British Library.

Library of Congress Cataloging-in-Publication Data

Russell, Betty G.
   Silent sisters: a study of homeless women / Betty G. Russell,
      p. cm.—(Series in health care for women)
   Includes bibliographical references.

   1. Homeless women—Maryland—Baltimore—Case studies.   I. Title.
II. Series.
HV4506.B35R87   1991
362.83′086942—dc20
                                              91-7401
                                               CIP

ISBN 1-56032-098-2
ISSN 1047-4005

Contents

Preface

In 1980, when I returned to Baltimore City as a permanent resident after 23 years of living in the suburbs, I noticed numerous street people in my travels through the city. Frequently, they were women. One day I was surprised to find a disheveled woman raving on a street corner not 50 feet from my apartment in a middle-class neighborhood. I became curious and concerned. Who were these women? What events had brought them to such pathetic circumstances? What did the future hold for them?

In 1983, as a student in an American Studies course in ethnography, I chose to study the "bag ladies" of Baltimore. I spent several months interviewing homeless women and volunteering at a daytime mission. I became even more concerned with the complexity and difficulties of these women's problems. During the following summer, I continued my investigations by living as a homeless woman for three days, sleeping in shelters, and eating in soup kitchens in Baltimore. This study is an extension of those preliminary investigations.

Silent Sisters is based on an ethnographic approach to cultural anthropology. Rather than studying homeless women from the cultural distance of the mainstream, I wanted to describe *their* point of view, both toward themselves and the mainstream. Participant observation, the methodology of ethnography, allows a researcher to learn about a group by observing the culture and then participating in it—an insider's, or emic view. I wanted to describe the world of these women, however, not only as an exercise in cultural analysis, but also to provide understanding that may help improve their situation or alleviate their problems. It is my hope that my voice may speak for them.

Acknowledgments

For help in this study I would like to thank the homeless women of Baltimore who, notwithstanding their own pain and fear, were willing to share their lives with me. At times they cried as they told their stories; we also laughed, for, in spite of their situation, they run the gamut of human emotion. In addition, the service providers were invaluable in assisting me: they gave their time, they provided me with helpful written materials, and they opened their doors to me. Carol Melvin and Renee Fries of the Women's Housing Coalition, Nancy Clark of the Park Avenue Lodge, Sister Pat McLaughlin of My Sister's Place, and Peggy Vick of the Salvation Army are women who have given their time and experience to help their silent sisters survive. My thanks also to those who directly or indirectly are involved with the homeless and gave their valuable time for interviews.

Dr. John Caughey, Department of American Studies at the University of Maryland, College Park, was instrumental in the development of this research. From my initial interest in this topic in his course in ethnography through my research and writing of the dissertation, John's patience and encouragement provided me with invaluable support. His suggestions helped me mold the original manuscript.

Holly Swartz's typing and proofreading were helpful in saving my time and energy for other tasks.

The publishing support of Ron Wilder and Carolyn Baker is much appreciated. They demystified the world of publishing for me. Special thanks to Amy Lyles Wilson for her excellent editing of the book. She helped me to clarify and to provide coherence.

I am grateful for family and friends who were always there and interested. Most of all I thank my husband Frank. When the task seemed overwhelming, his devotion and humor helped me immeasurably. His own visual statement of concern for the homeless has enriched all who have seen it.

INTRODUCTION

She sat in the corner of the large room, staring into space. Suddenly, her arms began to wave wildly and her face contorted and twisted into spasms. After 30 seconds or so, she again became still and resumed her trance-like state. I asked who she was. "She was a teacher in Baltimore City, her name is Betty, and she has recently been released from Springfield [a state mental hospital]," explained the woman in charge of the day shelter.

I teach in Baltimore County, and my name is Betty Russell. In my search for who the homeless women of Baltimore are, I found the answer on the first day I visited a shelter for homeless women: the homeless can be anyone. The memory of Betty is still vivid, for she was the first of many homeless women I have met during the past seven years.

Ada, for example, is between 55 and 65. Her head seems grotesquely misshapen on one side because of the huge mass of her grey-white hair, which she tries to cover with a scarf. Many of her teeth are missing and her face is deeply lined. Even in the warmth of a May evening she wears layers of clothes. Her legs are swollen and ulcerated, and her bare feet, propped on a box, are black with grime. She said she had been sleeping in a deserted house with dozens of cats, and the infected scratches on her legs bear testimony to her statement. Sitting on a metal chair, she waits for the Salvation Army canteen truck from which she will get her evening meal. She is one of Baltimore's "bag ladies."

Vanessa, a petite 36-year-old, is originally from Brooklyn, New York. For eight years, Vanessa was a prostitute, beginning as an expensive call girl and then "going to worse and worse houses [of prostitution]" because of the needle marks on her body from her drug addiction. On this February day she wears freshly-laundered jeans and a white sweatshirt. Her hair is shining clean in a short, curly, cut. She moves her hands frequently while she talks because she is nervous. But she wants to tell her story. "I want my family to know what happened to me," she says bitterly. A nurse before becoming a prostitute, she has just completed a refresher course in nursing and has a job in a hospital. Recovered from her drug and alcohol addictions, she presently lives in a transitional shelter.

Dorothy is in her forties, a little on the plump side, and very soft spoken. Neat and clean, she always wears slacks. She keeps her hair short and attractive and wears lipstick. She smokes nonfiltered cigarettes, as many as three or four packs a day. Her coughing racks her body and leaves her red-faced and gasping, but she continues to chain smoke. She has been between shelters and mental institutions for at least four years. Diagnosed as a schizophrenic, she is currently on medication. Dorothy smiles more these days, and her face lights with delight when she is complimented on her appearance. Laughter is now a part of her life. She is living in a long-term shelter for deinstitutionalized women that provides the supportive attention Dorothy needs.

Henrietta, with an ill-fitting golden brown wig sitting somewhat askew on her head, her face heavily lined for a woman just turned 51, sits in the day shelter and tries to hide the fact that she has no upper teeth. She says, "I'm fifty-one already. I didn't realize it. I didn't get any cards or anything." She has not been in touch with her two grown children for more than two years. She has been divorced twice. When asked who is responsible for her present situation, she replies, "That's what I'd like to know. I think I made a mistake, getting married the second time. My life's been goofed up ever since." An alcoholic just released from a detoxification unit, she will sleep at the Salvation Army emergency shelter this night.

These are sketches of some of the women in Baltimore, Maryland, who are part of the homeless population of the largest city in that state. Ada's appearance fits the stereotype that the majority of Americans recognize as that of a homeless woman, yet the other women described make up the estimated 350,000 to 3 million Americans who were homeless in 1990 (Speakers' Bureau, 1990). Although each of these women has shelter for the night, each is considered to be homeless.

To twentieth century Americans the word home has numerous definitions, but it connotes a shelter of some kind, usually a house. The terms *houseless* or *those without houses* might seem to be appropriate synonyms for homelessness. The words *homeless* or *homelessness* mean more than "those without homes." They are collective nouns that include a wide variety of people who have no permanent address. The majority of people unfamiliar with the problems of homelessness have believed that to be homeless means to live in the streets.

Homelessness is much more complex than that. Although the number of home-less who have been "counted" ranges from 250,000 to 3,000,000, neither figure reflects the people who are using makeshift quarters such as sleeping with friends, sharing the floor in a relative's apartment, doubling or tripling up until the landlord discovers them and they are evicted (Hopper, Baxter, Cox, & Klein, 1982). Another group of homeless moves from emergency shelter to emergency shelter, staying as long as they are allowed and then moving on to the next shelter. Still another group moves from emergency shelter into transi-tional shelter, which may last as long as a year. For some few, this may result in moving back into the mainstream. For many, it may mean once again moving to another shelter or in with friends or to a state hospital or detoxification unit until the cycle of homelessness begins again.

What has caused approximately somewhat less than + 1% of the U.S. population to be without homes (Auletta, 1982)? Homelessness in the United States existed prior to the 1980s. For example, the American Revolutionary War, the War of 1812, and the Civil War caused homelessness. Economic reces-sions and depressions also prompted Americans to leave their homes and mi-grate to what they believed were greener pastures. The Great Depression of this century resulted in tens of thousands of people crisscrossing the country, often living in their cars or trucks. Additionally, the lure of the open road has created an entire subculture of "homeless" men we have labeled *tramps.*

The homelessness of the last decade, however, has different causes. Most researchers, as well as those working in the field of homelessness, attribute the recent crisis in homelessness to lack of low-income housing, cutbacks in public assistance, deinstitutionalization, and unemployment (Hope & Young, 1984; Rossi, 1989).

The majority of today's homeless are not the bums, derelicts, or romanti-cized wanderers of the open road, yet the homelessness of present day Ameri-cans is unique in at least one way. From Huckleberry Finn and Jack London to sociological researchers Nels Anderson and Douglas Harper, male tramps or homeless men have been the subject of fiction, research, and mythology for more than 100 years. Not so with homeless American women, although they represent the fastest growing number of the homeless (Hopper & Hamberg, 1984). Studies of homeless women are needed to fill the gap. Even in 1991 the information about homeless women is scant, and the focus of the media has been on men and "families" who are staying in shelters, even though the majority of these "families" are headed by single women (Stengel, 1986). Current research that has focused on women has concentrated on the bag ladies (Rousseau, 1981) and/or the deinstitutionalized women such as that of Bassuk (1986), Bassuk, Rubin, and Lauriat (1984), and Breakey (1985). Roper (1988) believes that the deinstitutionalized comprise only a small portion of the home-less.

This study focuses on the homeless women in Baltimore who live for any length of time in shelters or missions run by religious organizations or public agencies. At the time of this study the women were residents of such shelters. Although I was concerned with the important questions of how women got into this situation and how they sometimes got out, the focus of the study was on the daily lives of these women. Once a woman was without permanent shelter, what strategies did she use to survive? Where did a woman find food? What arrangements did she make for shelter? Where did she obtain clothing? Where did she bathe and launder her clothing? How and where did she fill the hours of her days? What possessions did she take with her when she became homeless? How did she view the agencies with whom she came in contact? How did she view herself and other homeless women? What were her hopes, fears, and dreams? What attitudes did she bring with her from the mainstream, and what attitudes did she change?

In exploring these questions I was also concerned with broader issues, such as to what extent homeless women have developed a specific culture or subculture. A culture is distinguished by a more or less distinctive set of customary activities or behavior patterns and a more or less distinctive shared language or argot that distinguish it from other groups (Singer, 1968). Many theorists and researchers have also argued that culture involves a discrete set of beliefs, values, and concepts—a meaning system—that lies behind patterns of behavior. Robert A. LeVine (1984), a cultural theorist, has defined culture as "a shared organization of ideas that includes the intellectual, moral, and aesthetic standards prevalent in a community, and the meanings of communicative actions" (p. 67). James Spradley and David W. McCurdy (1980) have used this definition: "Culture is the acquired knowledge that people use to interpret experience and to generate social behavior" (p. 5). Both of these definitions are applicable to this study.

American society is generally understood to have a widely-shared mainstream culture and also to be a pluralistic culture. There are systems of knowledge and patterns of behavior both within the mainstream and its fringes. Many subcultures have been identified and described, such as those of the Amish, Mormons, gangs of delinquents, drug users, ethnic groups, and male tramps. In this study I was concerned with the manner and extent to which homeless women of Baltimore had developed a subculture—that is, a distinctive system of language connected to values and meanings that are different from those found in the mainstream. I was also concerned with how this system compares to that of the much-studied subculture of homeless men. Of particular interest was the extent to which women were not antagonistic toward or disaffiliated from mainstream culture.

I was also concerned with the role that gender plays in the homelessness of women. One area of interest was the view that homeless women have of themselves and each other as women. Carol Gilligan (1982), a feminist psychologist, observed that, for women "Identity is defined in a context of relationship and judged by a standard of responsibility and care" (p. 160). Because many homeless women leave their everyday relationships behind when they are displaced, on what basis do they then judge themselves? I was also concerned with what role gender plays in the similarities and differences between the subcultures of homeless men and women. An additional focus was the extent to which homeless women live in a female world; that is, one that primarily contains other homeless women and female service providers, and the impact this may have on the daily lives of homeless women.

The organization, ideology, and policies of government agencies, such as the police department and the Department of Social Services, and particularly those of the shelter providers, also impact on the lives of the homeless. Other questions that this research attempted to answer are how these agencies viewed the homeless women, what they were trying to do for them, and what intentional and unintentional consequences these policies had on homeless women. An additional point of view that has been included is that of mainstream America and the government policies that reflect its attitudes. There is considerable ambivalence in our country toward the homeless. Shifts in attitudes and governmental policies have had and will continue to have important consequences for support agencies and the lives of homeless women.

Finally, I sought to explore the extent to which the stereotypes of homeless women are accurate. One view, for example, sees the majority of homeless women as mentally ill. Another view holds that they are substance abusers. Still another view sees them as irresponsible parasites who live off of the generosity of mainstream America. To what extent are these stereotypes true, and what are the implications of these findings?

The majority of the women who participated in this study availed themselves of food, clothing, and shelter from service providers, and it was in this way that I came into contact with them. During the time of the interviews, from June 1986 through October 1987, the women were residing in one emergency shelter, five transitional shelters, and one day shelter in Baltimore, Maryland. I was a volunteer at the day shelter for four months, with the Women's Housing Coalition for a year, and visited the Salvation Army Shelter (an emergency shelter) several times a month for a year and a half. In addition, I have been a weekly volunteer on the Salvation Army canteen truck since 1986. I have continued contact with homeless women as a volunteer with the Women's Housing Coalition. With the exception of my own personal experience in living in shelters for several days in 1983, I always explained to shelter providers why I wanted to interview the women and obtained permission of the directors of the shelters to do so. With their cooperation, I was able to observe not only the residents, but also to watch the interaction between the service providers and their clients and to interview the service providers as well.

The methodology used in this study was ethnographic. In James Spradley's *The Ethnographic Interview* (1979), the author used Malinowski's definition of the goal of ethnography: "to grasp the native's point of view, his relation to life, to realize *his* vision of *his* world," (emphasis in original, p. 3). The role of the researcher as participant-observer-interviewer in collecting data and analyzing the results to write an ethnography can contribute significantly to the study of female homelessness. The increase in the number of homeless men and women in recent years has lead to an increase in research on this population, but the majority of studies have been from a social science, psychological, psychiatric, or demographic perspective (e.g., Crystal, 1984; Bahr & Garrett, 1976; Bassuk, 1986; Rossi, 1989). The ethnographic approach differs from these approaches because the ethnographer asks the insider to describe and explain his or her activities, experiences, and knowledge. Having observed and questioned, the ethnographer can then participate in the activities of the group being studied.

The women I first interviewed in 1983 repeatedly said to me, "If you want to know what it's like to be homeless, you have to do this yourself." The three days I spent as a homeless woman enabled me to put into practice what I had learned in preliminary interviews with homeless women. I passed myself off as a homeless woman and was accepted by both other homeless women and shelter providers. With the help of Sister Pat McLaughlin (who was the only one who knew I was not homeless) at My Sister's Place, I stayed at two shelters and ate in soup kitchens without being challenged. My sister residents at the two shelters shared information as well as soap and nail polish. I had a small notebook in my skirt pocket, and after leaving the shelter in the morning I would write down my impressions and any dialogue that I could recall.

My experiences as a volunteer allowed me to earn the trust and acceptance of many of the women. By holding babies, pouring coffee, and chatting with the women, I soon was able to disclose that I was writing a book on the problems and needs of women who have to stay in shelters. I then asked the women to complete a questionnaire using only their initials as a code for me (see Appendixes 1 and 2 for complete questionnaires and results). If they answered question 27 with a "yes" (Have you ever lived in the streets? If so, would you be willing to discuss it with me?), I requested an interview with them. Because the women at the Salvation Army shelter only stayed for the maximum length of 21 days, most of the women I interviewed were residents of transitional shelters. The stay in a transitional shelter might be as long as 1 year and the women would be available when I needed follow-up interviews. In the in-depth interviews I asked questions that would help the women portray their lives before they became homeless, which in many cases involved lengthy descriptions of their childhoods as well as their recent pasts. I focused on their present lives and how they lived from day to day, but I also asked about their hopes and dreams, and what they saw as their futures. To protect their identities, I asked the women to rename themselves, choosing names they wished they could have been named originally (this accounts for two Elizabeths in the study). I had formal interviews with 22 women, and 10 were reinterviewed at least once. Nine of the 22 women allowed me to tape their interviews; the other 13 allowed me to make extensive notes during the interviews. I had informal conversational interviews with approximately 50 to 60 women. I also observed many women in a variety of roles, such as residents at shelters, diners at soup kitchens, participants in social activities (e.g., art class, cookout), and mothers with children, as well as others. One hundred women answered the questionnaire in full or in part. Throughout this book, the women interviewed will be called "the women." The women who answered only the questionnaire will be called "the questionnaire group."

The format of the book is organized to include a brief history of homelessness in the United States, an overview of tramp culture, a description of the lives of the women from their entrance into homelessness until they rejoin the mainstream, and recommendations for changes in policies that deal with homeless women.

Betty, the former teacher, and her homeless sisters have not disappeared from Baltimore or from the national scene. On the contrary, their numbers are increasing (Rossi, 1989). Through an approach that allows the women to speak through my voice, it is hoped that they will no longer be silent, and that all of us can have a clearer understanding of what homelessness is like for women.

2

ACTIONS AND ATTITUDES

Homelessness is not unique to either the twentieth century or to the United States. The homeless poor have been present in many world societies, including early phases of Western culture. For example, in the Old Testament book of Ruth, which tells the story of a homeless woman, the Jews left the gleanings of their harvests for the poor, and in the New Testament, Christ sanctified the poor by equating them with Himself. The necessity for delineating the treatment of the poor implies that there was neglect of and hostility toward the poor, depending on the social or cultural conditions of the time.

This ambivalence has continued throughout the history of Western society and exists in the United States today. The attitudes of mainstream America have shifted between harsh regulations and sternness on one hand, and selfless generosity and compassion on the other. Today's attitudes are hardly new. Homelessness has existed in America since the settlement of the English colonies (Hope & Young, 1986; Rossi, 1989). The travelers to this land, homeless themselves, brought with them laws and attitudes toward homelessness characteristic of European cultures and the Judeo-Christian teachings on which they were based. These included hospices for the poor as well as the branding of vagrants. Most relevant to the settlement of the colonies and subsequent laws dealing with the poor were the English concepts of the "deserving" and "undeserving" poor—those unable to work and those unwilling to work (Dolgoff & Feldstein, 1980). Public assistance was available in all of the colonies by the time of the American Revolution, but specific requirements had to be met (Crouse, 1986).

The American Revolutionary War caused a new kind of poor and homeless person—the female camp followers of both the British and American armies (Blumenthal, 1952). Although the exact number of these women is not known, the number of women varied considerably at different times and in different localities. The camp followers for the British consisted in some cases of wives of officers, but more often they were washerwomen, wives and mistresses of ordinary soldiers, and prostitutes. There were also indentured female servants, either runaways or those who had served their time. Many of the women who followed the American army were refugees who fled before the British advance and traveled with the army, washing and mending the soldiers' clothes and tending the wounded. The soldiers viewed them as welcome assets. When the armies disbanded at the end of the war, the women melted back into the mainstream (Blumenthal, 1952).

The Civil War created another set of homeless people for both the North and the South. Many veterans and their families moved west to settle on land grants or to build the transcontinental railroad lines. The Depression of 1873 not only caused massive unemployment, but also homelessness. Many of these followed the railroads to work as miners, loggers, and farmhands (Gimlin, 1982). The temporary or seasonal nature of many of these jobs caused men to drift from town to town and by 1877 "tramps" were perceived as a problem. Often the tramps drifted back to large urban centers. Paul T. Ringenbach's (1973) research of tramps and reformers in New York City from 1873 to 1916 found that in 1874-75 in New York City, 435,000 people were lodged in police stations and in 1877 alone, 1 million people were arrested for vagrancy. The terms *hobo* and *panhandler* also appeared at this time.

As long as the number of tramps in America remained small, they were not viewed as a threat. Before 1873 the tramp had become a familiar figure in the countryside as he panhandled money or did a few chores in exchange for a meal. As the number of tramps increased, however, public attitudes changed and "cures for trampism" began to appear. Ringenbach (1973) listed a number of "remedies" culled from the popular literature and media of the day. A gun company advertised a shotgun named the "Tramp Terror"; the *Chicago Tribune* suggested sprinkling a tramp's food with strychnine or arsenic; *Century Magazine* featured an illustration titled "Timber Lesson," in which boys and men were depicted whipping a tramp with sticks and brooms; and a public official in Westchester County, New York, proposed placing a tramp in a tank, flooding it with water and letting him pump it out to keep himself from drowning, an idea that was not utilized (Allsop, 1967; Ringenbach, 1973). Although Ringenbach notes that the actual implementation of these ideas was rare, such recommendations do indicate the attitudes of some Americans toward the tramp.

The number of tramps declined during World War I when manpower became scarce on the homefront, but the numbers rose again after the war because of returning veterans (Wallace, 1965). In 1924 the first of Norman Rockwell's tramps appeared on the cover of *The Saturday Evening Post*. Two other fictionalized tramps also appeared as cartoon characters during this period—Weary Willie and Happy Hooligan (Allsop, 1967). According to one historian of tramp culture, Kenneth Allsop (1967), this popularization of the hobo "depersonalized him, disqualified him from concern, and made him invisible," (pp. 146-147). The most famous tramp of all time flickered to life on the screen in the person of Charley Chaplin's tramp in 1915 in *The Tramp,* and five other tramp films followed this debut (Allsop, 1967). The American public might not want a real tramp knocking at its door for a handout, but it opened its heart to Chaplin's depiction.

Although male tramps were an established subculture of American society by World War I, women on the road were an anomaly (Box-Car Bertha, 1975). The Great Depression altered not only life in the mainstream, but also life on the road. The Depression caused changes in the conventions of who could ride the rails, for although some few women had traveled with tramps prior to this period, Box-Car Bertha (1975) estimated that thousands of women now joined the men traveling the country. A woman who rode the rails herself, she estimated that there were 13,600 women, "sisters of the road, as the men call us," in 1937 (p. 9). She further observed about the women, "I've decided that the most frequent reason they leave home is economic and that they usually come from broken or poverty-stricken homes," (p. 16). The women with whom Bertha traveled made ends meet through stealing, begging, hustling, or with help from the welfare agencies. If the weather was good they slept outside with the men and bathed in the lavatories at libraries or other public buildings.

Estimates of the number of women on the road ranged from 14,482 in the 1933 census to 250,000 (Crouse, 1986). Joan Crouse, a social historian, has profiled the lives of women on the road during the Great Depression. Agencies of that period would usually return the woman to her hometown. Rather than go to the agencies for help, the woman would provide sexual favors to a man in exchange for food, shelter, and protection. Often she would allow herself to reach such a stage of mental and physical exhaustion before asking for help that she would have to be hospitalized. For the most part women were absent even in breadlines because they had been used to relief in the almshouse or in the privacy of their homes, not in public. Tradition dictated that a woman should be protected and that no matter how difficult the situation, a family member would provide shelter. When women did take to the road, they had the same needs as men—food and shelter—but, unlike the men, had no hobo customs or tradition to help them adapt to their new situation. Crouse (1986) cited Walter C. Reckless, author of "Why Women Become Hoboes" for the February 1934, issue of *The American Mercury* who stated, "Women have not had time to build up their own communal life," (p. 111).

The government relief programs of the Roosevelt administration in the 1930s and the onset of World War II saw an almost total end to the problem of American homelessness (Allsop, 1967). The war economy provided jobs for both men and women, and men were also needed for the armed services. The post-war boom continued to keep the number of homeless at a level acceptable to the public—the alcoholics and bums who inhabited the skid rows of American cities, (those areas of cities where bums congregated), or rode the freights from "jungle" to "jungle" (camps outside populated areas where bums camped for short periods of time) (Allsop, 1967). Howard M. Bahr's (1973) study of skid rows revealed that the majority of homeless men in this post-war period were usually older white men with chronic ailments who had spent years living on the edges of society. Homelessness seemed to be on the verge of extinction not only because of the economic boom, but also because urban renewal had revitalized many of the areas where skid rows were located (Salerno, Hopper, & Baxter, 1984). The War on Poverty of the 1960s increased the optimistic forecast that skid rows would disappear as pension benefits and welfare benefits improved (Wallace, 1965). Yet, during the 1980s the United States saw the greatest number of homeless since the Great Depression, an alarming proportion of whom were women (Rossi, 1989).

Once again there is a dichotomy in the attitudes of Americans toward the poor and the homeless in our country. Americans have responded to the plight of the homeless in personal ways. Lawyers and law students in several cities have volunteered their time (Crockett, 1988) to operate legal clinics that represent the homeless. College students from more than 50 colleges across the country held a Teach-In to address the needs of the homeless in their communities (National Coalition for the Homeless, 1987). Although Hands Across America in 1986 did not reach its $100 million goal, it did raise $16 million for the homeless, and an estimated 4.9 million people turned out to join hands in symbolic support of aid to America's homeless ("Millions Form Human Chain," 1986, May 26). Additionally, thousands of people have served as volunteers in shelters and soup kitchens throughout the country even before President Bush's "thousand points of light" answer to appeals for more spending on social programs.

Yet some Americans respond in different ways that vary according to the vagaries of popular culture and the media. A local newspaper carried an article at the beginning of 1987 describing what was "in" and what was "out" for 1987; hunger was "out" and homelessness was "in." In 1987, movies stars and Congressmen slept with the homeless on the Capitol's steps on a winter night ("Actors," 1987, April). Commercially, a California businessman offered "bag lady grams" (singing telegrams with the messenger dressed as a bag lady) (Karp, 1986), and a national catalog featured a cover photo of a soft sculpture bag lady seated on a small park bench for a cost of $290, including the bench. A few years ago Bloomingdale's featured the "bag lady look." In 1986, Lucille Ball starred in a television movie titled *Stone Pillow,* the story of a bag lady living in New York. In some circles homelessness has been chic; in others, it has been good business.

In addition, there are many political dimensions for Americans when dealing with homelessness. Because it is necessary to have an address when registering to vote, most homeless people do not vote because they have no addresses to list. This lowers their power to elect officials. However, their presence, in middle-class neighborhoods, shopping centers, and at tourist sites often causes consternation to voting citizens and may prompt calls to the police (Dennis Hill, Director of Public Information, Baltimore City Police Department, personal communication, Feb. 2, 1987). Often the problem to the citizen is minimal compared to that of the homeless person. On a cold March night in Baltimore, a shivering, starving man stood hunched over, drinking cup after cup of soup handed to him from the Salvation Army canteen truck. A middle-class businessman approached the volunteer in the truck and demanded that the truck move elsewhere because, he complained, these men always left their paper soup bowls on the steps of his office building and urinated in the alley behind his property. This man's hostility was based on his personal experience with a specific group of homeless men. But he exemplified a person who thinks in stereotypes, for his parting comment was, "These people do 'this everywhere. I've seen them do it all over downtown." If the homeless are viewed as stereotypes rather than as individuals, they can too easily be relegated to the status of "a problem."

Across the nation, "solutions" for the homeless "problem" have included the following: in Fort Lauderdale, a city commissioner suggested putting rat poison on the top of garbage (he later retracted this and recommended the use of chlorine bleach instead) (Salerno, Hopper, & Baxter, 1984); in Winnemucca, Nevada, policemen placed the homeless in city garbage pits or drove them into the desert and left them; in Greenwich Village, barbed wire was placed over steam grates where the homeless often sleep (Leo, 1985); in Reno, Nevada, the state gave the homeless directions or one-way tickets to other states (Hope & Young, 1986); Phoenix made all of its trash city property and jailed anyone who stole "public property" (Salerno et al., 1984); Atlanta, Miami, and other cities placed "No Trespassing" signs in city parks; New Orleans arrested people standing in welfare lines on vagrancy charges (Hope & Young, 1986); in Santa Cruz, California, off-duty policemen wore TROLL BUSTER t-shirts in a city that called homeless people trolls; in San Diego, a shelter was burned by an arsonist; and a 35-year-old drifter in Santa Barbara, California, was found shot to death, and a flyer was circulated threatening more violence to the homeless (Leo, 1985). A 42-year-old California stockbroker and city council member commented, "It's an understandable and common reaction for any animal society to rid itself of those who aren't productive," (Leo, 11 March 1985, p. 68). Mitch Snyder, who was an ardent and prominent advocate for the homeless before his death in 1990, testified before the U.S. Senate Committee on Appropriations:

The homeless—particularly the physically and mentally disabled—are our human refuse, remnants of a culture that assigns a pathologically high value to independence and productivity. America is a land where you are what you consume and produce (United States Congress, Senate Committee on Appropriations, Street People, 1983, p. 7).

By reducing the homeless to the level of garbage, trolls, and undesirables, mainstream America can read of such violations against human rights and remain silent. One middle-class woman made the following comment to this author: "We Americans like our charity donations to go to the starving in Africa. We don't want to see, face-to-face, pain and suffering." Homeless Americans are in our main streets, and some are even on our doorsteps. We can see them face-to-face. By using the stereotype of homeless people, however, we can turn our faces away by offering simplistic solutions as did a writer of a letter to *The Baltimore Sun.* His thinking can be summarized as follows:

- the homeless have jobs available to them in the classifieds, but they just don't apply for employment;
- all of the homeless have dropped out of school;
- homeless women have deliberately had children they knew they could not afford;
- many of the homeless abuse drugs and alcohol;
- the homeless who are mentally ill all belong in mental institutions;
- our money is wasted on so many people who don't deserve compassion. ("Blaming Reagan," 1986, p. A6)

Further compounding the problem is the controversy over the number of homeless in the United States (Rossi, 1989). There are several problems in gathering statistics on the homeless population. First, many homeless are hidden: living in abandoned buildings, sleeping in parks or doorways, and moving from one site to another. They do not wish to be counted or contacted in any way. Second, some will not admit to being homeless. Instead, they will explain that they are staying with a friend or are only homeless for a night until they can move into a new place. Third, the number of homeless varies with the seasons, the economy, and even the time of the month, because welfare money tends to run out sometime around the twentieth of the month, often resulting in eviction (Cuomo, 1983).

The battle over the correct number of homeless in the United States has enormous economic portent, both on the local and the federal levels, for the number of homeless will affect the forms and amounts of assistance that will be offered to the homeless (Rossi, 1989). At the National Governors' Association meeting in 1983 in Portland, Maine, Governor Mario Cuomo of New York in his report, *1933/1983—Never Again,* stated, "Ultimately, collective responsibility for the dependent and disabled must be rooted in the principled participation of government," (p. 69). The National Coalition for the Homeless recently stated in its report, *National Neglect/National Shame* (1986), that local agencies and volunteer organizations can no longer carry the financial burden for relieving the plight of the homeless and the hungry. Local news articles reporting the closing of shelters and soup kitchens are examples of what happens when money runs out (Greene, 1986). In fiscal year 1986, Baltimore, Boston, Chicago, New York, Philadelphia, and Seattle spent a total of $100,270,000 on emergency food and shelter, but this did not meet the need (Greater Baltimore Shelter Network [GBSN], 1986). Clearly, the number of homeless is important, for the homeless are an important financial factor. The increasing number of the homeless has attracted the attention of reporters, which in turn has resulted in more public awareness ("Housing Now," 1989) and pressure ("McKinney Act Reauthorized and Expanded," 1990) on both local and federal governments to increase spending on food and shelter for the homeless. Nevertheless, the homeless continue to die in our streets every year.

3

THE TRAMP VERSUS THE BAG LADY

THE OPEN ROAD VERSUS THE CITYSCAPE

In 1965, Samuel E. Wallace, in *Skid Row as a Way of Life,* wrote that there had been more than 150 studies on skid row and its members during the hundred years that skid rows had existed. The majority of these works focused on men. One of the reasons for this is that the majority of the inhabitants of skid row have been men. Gerald R. Garrett and Howard M. Bahr (1973), sociologists who have done extensive research on skid row populations, have noted that historically there has been "little or no public interest" in homeless women because "ecological concentrations of homeless or alcoholic women have not been perceived as threatening the social order or as neighborhood problems as have some homeless men in the past" (p. 1229). In order to understand the phenomenon of homeless women in the 1980s it is necessary to contrast the subculture of the skid row/homeless man with that of the skid row/homeless woman.

An examination of American literature reveals the romanticized treatment of the homeless man or tramp. Huck Finn and Jim, Jack London, Lennie and George in *Of Mice and Men,* Francis Phelan in *Ironweed,* Jack Kerouac's poetry, and John Denver's "On the Road Again" are all characterizations of the freedom and glory of the open road. As Crouse (1986) has written:

In the tradition of American legends, the "man on the move" has generally been a larger than life hero. . . . Each such hero was in effect "a migrant" or "a transient." (p. 1)

The pejorative terms were almost never used and the more romantic terms such as *pioneer, frontiersman,* and *adventurer* were preferred. The only deterrent to this romance with the open road was when the numbers of homeless drifters seemed to threaten communities.

Eric Monkkonen's (1984) analysis of tramping divided the history into two major segments: from the end of the Civil War to 1920, which marked the era of the industrial tramp, those who traveled the road from job to job, and from 1920 to the present, which has marked the era of the homeless tramp. The period to 1920 accounts for the "subculture" or trampism that has been the subject of so much research. Although there was wide diversity in the lives of homeless men during this period, there were enough shared characteristics to form a subculture that created a unique language and a distinctive lifestyle—that of the tramp and skid row.

Skid rows began appearing across the country after the Civil War. The name, however, came from Seattle, Washington, where a street inhabited by lumberjacks was used to skid logs to a sawmill, and which comprised a community of brothels, saloons, and flophouses (Gimlin, 1982; Wallace, 1965). The name came to mean "a district in the city where there is a concentration of substandard hotels and rooming houses charging very low rates and catering primarily to men with low incomes" (Bogue, 1963, p. 1). These areas were usually located near rail yards, trucking depots, waterfronts, or factory districts (Schneider, 1986). Skid rows were comprised almost solely of white men (Bahr & Garrett, 1976; Hopper & Hamberg, 1984). Living together and traveling together, the men developed dress, behavior, and language that were distinctly outside the mainstream. Josiah Flynt (1972), one of the researchers to document the language of tramping, compiled a glossary in *Tramping With Tramps* that included such terms as *bull, Bo,* and *stiff.* James Spradley's (1970) ethnography of drunks in Seattle, Washington, revealed the use of these very terms to mean "a policeman," "a hobo," and "a fellow." One did not simply become a tramp by being homeless; one had to learn the subculture of tramping.

The period from the late 1920s to the 1940s, the Great Depression, saw a drop in the numbers of "professional" tramps. By the 1950s, skid rows were the haunts of perennial derelicts, "populated by casualties of poverty, pathology, old age, character deficiencies, or alcohol dependency" (Hopper & Hamberg, 1984, p. 16). Wallace (1965) states that the estimated number of people living on skid rows in 41 cities of the United States in 1950 was less than 100,000. The days of the "Knights of the Road," as tramps had been nicknamed, seemed to be almost over.

Donald J. Bogue (1963) conducted extensive studies of skid rows in various cities in the United States in the 1960s. His research discloses numerous characteristics of homeless men. For example, most had no family life, were poor and worked irregularly for low pay, and had "acute societal and interpersonal problems" (p. 2). One of the questions asked by Bogue concerned the happiness of the homeless men's parents. More than 70% claimed their parents' marriage was either "unusually happy" or "happy," and only 13% reported that the marriage was "unhappy" or "very unhappy" (p. 332). Three out of five had fathers who were operatives, craftsman, or unskilled nonfarm laborers, and 80% reported favorable treatment from their fathers, although 20% had fathers who were heavy drinkers. The men almost unanimously absolved their mothers of blame for their plight, and less than 1% reported a mother who was a heavy drinker. Only 15% said that there was substantial domestic discord in their homes, and 23% came from broken homes. Bogue also found that 86% had worked during the year preceding the interview, indicating that the men were employable.

Some of the most interesting information that Bogue learned, for the purpose of this study, was in the area of homeless men and their relationships with women. Forty-five percent of the men Bogue interviewed had never married and almost all who had married were either separated or divorced. The majority of men who remained single did so out of preference, and Bogue concluded that in comparison with the general population these men had a low interest in marriage and sex and that they preferred prostitutes to wives. Bogue's research also revealed the men's attitudes toward women and marriage. If they had been married, their marriages had lasted a median of seven years and many were approaching middle age when they left their wives. Forty percent held themselves responsible for the breakup and 43% stated incompatibility as the cause. Thirty-nine percent said being a good housekeeper was the most important trait that a wife could have. When asked to name their aspirations, Bogue's interviewees named in order of preference a job or a better job, health, and money to escape skid row. One of Bogue's observations follows:

Almost any American citizen, if denied work opportunities for a prolonged span of time, would end up in the skid row soup line unless saved from this fate by a family or by some program of social legislation. (p. 197)

Ten years after Bogue's study, Howard Bahr (1973) found similar characteristics in the skid row men he studied: most were white and only about half had been married and for short periods of time. In addition, 40–60% of the men were natives of the city or region where their skid row was located, and fewer than 10% slept in missions. It is important to note that from the 1950s to the 1970s the majority of men were not sleeping in the streets but were housed in flophouses, jails (after being arrested for vagrancy), or municipal lodging houses in addition to the small percentage who stayed at missions. Bahr's explanation for the reluctance of the men to seek shelter from charities is the "facade of penitence" that many charitable institutions seem to demand (p. 138). Other characteristics of skid row men were described by Samuel Wallace (1965) in *Skid Row as a Way of Life:*

> *The skid rower does not bathe, eat regularly, dress respectably, marry or raise children, attend school, vote, own property, or regularly live in the same place. He does little work of any kind. (p. 144)*

However, James Spradley (1970) noted that, "The urban nomad culture is characterized by mobility, alienation, poverty, and a unique set of survival strategies" (p. 253). Additionally, he noted that almost half the men he studied in Seattle had been married and supported families; most had worked and some were receiving pensions; and that a few had even attended college. Spradley's research involved men who were arrested for vagrancy and public drunkenness, a sample not representative of all men on skid row.

The subculture of homeless men is different from mainstream America in other respects. One aspect that can differ from subculture to subculture is that of time. Harry Murray (1986), an applied anthropologist using participant observation in men's shelters in a northeastern city, has argued that even time is different in the streets. Although the person in the streets cannot escape the linear time of the dominant culture of the United States, he tends to view time as cyclical; that is, a daily cycle that depends on soup kitchen and shelter schedules, a monthly cycle in which the arrival of welfare or veteran's checks determines where one sleeps, and a seasonal cycle in which weather is an important factor for survival.

Another difference between homeless men and the mainstream is the emphasis on material possessions. Homeless men tend to carry very little with them. Spradley (1970) has observed that in the world of the urban nomad, the man with the fewest possessions is the most respected, but that the loss of those possessions such as "rings, watches, money, wallets, identification papers, address books, and clothing" symbolizes the loss of the man's identity (p. 144). Similarly, Harvey Siegal (1974), in a participant observation study of residents of single room occupancy hotels (SRO's) in New York, reported that a manager's ordering the resident to leave resulted in a few possessions being thrown into shopping bags—"not the stuff from which an identity can be forged" (p. 300). The men I observed week after week from the Salvation Army canteen truck in Baltimore carried all of their belongings in several plastic shopping bags or in backpacks, the exceptions being a man who pushed a shopping cart overflowing with his possessions. It is logical that men on the move do not wish to be bothered with possessions that may be difficult and burdensome to carry. It is one of the reasons that the homeless wear layers of clothing in the summer, for otherwise they would have to carry the clothes in bags. One of the indispensable items that a street person needs and carries is a blanket because it can keep him or her from freezing to death. In my experience, it is one of the most frequently requested items by the men who eat from the Salvation Army canteen.

In 1981, Douglas Harper (1982) traveled the rails from Chicago to Washington state and used ethnographic methods to study the lives of the men he met on the road. Those men taught him what to carry with him, how to hop a train, where to stay along the way, how to handle himself: in short, how to survive. On the road and in the streets, survival skills are shared. In the streets of Baltimore, for example, the men who eat at the Salvation Army canteen can be overheard telling a new man where he can stay and where he can eat. Numerous accounts of male reporters who have lived for brief periods of time in the streets relate how they obtain survival information from other men in the streets (Flynn, 1986; Harper, 1982). Repeatedly, many men confess to liking street life. Spradley (1970) stated that there are men who "out of desire or habit" will always be tramps (p. 261). Ramsey Flynn (1986) who spent several days living as a homeless man, reported in *Baltimore* magazine that:

> *I feel I have a right to homestead in this cubbyhole; no need for rent. . . . I don't need money; free food is plentiful. . . . I don't need clothes; the missionaries have offered them to me repeatedly. (p. 135)*

Douglas Harper in *Good Company* (1982) also longed to return to the open road and the freedom that it represented, even though he was married and the father of a child. One man interviewed by a local paper (Greene, 1986) stated that he had spent much of his adult life wandering throughout the country working only temporarily in order to earn a few dollars. In another interview, (Frece. 1986, p. E6) a homeless man stated that he had been drifting more than half his life and that he liked "traveling around."

The studies of Bogue (1963) and Bahr (1973) were from an outsider's point of view; that is, these researchers used questionnaires and other methods to compile their data. Spradley (1970) and Harper (1982) used an insider's method. Interviewees may answer questions differently depending on their audiences. Erving Goffman (1959) used the analogy of "frontstage" and "backstage" to identify the two areas in which informants can respond. "Frontstage," the "player" gives a performance that the audience expects, while "backstage" the "player" can be himself. Spradley (1970), Harper (1983), Siegal (1974), and Murray (1986) were able to view tramps and urban nomads "backstage," thus providing insights on the values and attitudes of male tramps.

Undoubtedly, these studies do not reflect the majority opinion, but they lend credence to the myth that for some men life on the road is an adventure.

INVISIBLE WOMEN

In the early 1980s the bag lady began to appear in the media. A woman, surrounded by her shopping bags, rummaging through trash containers, strangely dressed, and, most importantly, alone, she became the stereotype for all homeless women. She was considered a new phenomena, a product of the 1970s. Her sisters of the past century were unknown and her sisters of the present were few in number, but just like her. She did not have a language that had existed for almost a century, she had not had fictional tales nor songs written about her, and she had not been studied by anyone. If she had existed at all on paper, it had been as a shadow at the edge of the male world of skid rows and homelessness. Bahr and Garrett (1976), writing about skid row inhabitants, have observed that women would be ignored even more in all kinds of research except that they are more often at home than husbands and are the informants on family and consumer preferences. Alix Kates Shulman (Rousseau, 1981) wrote in the introduction to *Shopping Bag Ladies,* a collection of oral histories, that women are ignored in a society in which they have little power because they are considered unimportant. Thus in the field of research, homeless women, for all practical purposes, are invisible. Yet the passing references to women in the male world of skid rows has yielded information that provides a sketchy background to contrast with that of homeless men.

Homeless women have not been romanticized as have homeless men. The word *tramp* has a different connotation when applied to a woman. At the turn of the century when tramping was at its peak, women on the road were known as "women hoboes" or "women adrift" (Weiner, 1984). Lynn Weiner's essay (1984) "Sisters of the Road" in *Walking to Work,* traced the history of these two groups of women and provides valuable insights into their life-styles. The women hoboes were considered unredeemable—deviants who were looking for adventure. The women adrift consisted of females who traveled the country looking for work and who were worthy of being helped. The women hoboes had broken from a woman's place, which was characterized by "dependency, domesticity, submission, and the other female virtues" (p. 172). The women adrift were expected to work only until "marriage would reestablish their domestic identity" (p. 172). The predominant fear was that these young women who moved to large cities looking for work as clerks, sales girls, and millworkers were living without moral guidance, which would ultimately endanger society. As a result of this fear, and based on the belief that these women were redeemable, reformers established transient boarding houses, and travelers' aid organizations narrowed their focus from men to women and children.

The women hoboes were considered aberrations even by the male tramps.

Newspaper articles of the period reveal the low esteem in which they were held. For example, the women were often harrassed sexually by tramps and Weiner (1984) attributed this to the cloak of respectability that these women had lost when they took to the road. Some of the women chose to cross dress to protect themselves and some even passed themselves off as men. Another method was to trade their sexual favors and domestic skills for protection. Although outside the pale of respectable womanhood, some women reflected the mainstream of society by bartering their skills of washing and mending clothes and cooking. Weiner also traces the lives of women hoboes in the Depression, when they were joined by a flood of women who were on the road out of necessity, not by choice. The later legislation of this decade, such as the Federal Transient Program, has been credited with effectively reducing the numbers of women transients. By the end of the Depression they were no longer considered to be a problem.

When the women hoboes reached cities, they often stayed on skid rows. There were, however, other women who lived on skid rows, although few studies have been done of them. In the nineteenth century brothels were located on skid rows and Weiner (1984) stated that these are mentioned in the literature of the period. Some of the prostitutes were homeless women who temporarily sought shelter in the brothels until they moved on to other areas. Alcohol was also associated with the women on skid row (Weiner, 1984). By the twentieth century the reform movements against alcohol and prostitution had helped depict women and children as victims and as objects of charitable giving (Blumberg, Shipley, & Barsky, 1978). This helped reduce the number of women on skid row, but not all women left skid row and rejoined the mainstream. In the 1970s when Garrett and Bahr (1973, 1976) conducted their studies of skid row women, they found that alcohol played a significant role in their lives. Bogue (1963) reported that prostitutes were found near the taverns and cheap hotels of skid rows.

THE GENDER GAP AND A MATTER OF ATTITUDES

Other than in the Depression, when female transients were seen as a part of a national problem of unemployment, large numbers of women living in the streets or applying to shelters for help have been unknown in this country. This has also been a reason for the lack of research on homeless women until the 1970s, when the increase was so significant that it could not be ignored (Rossi, 1989). Recent inquiries and reports from service providers, however, indicate that homelessness for women is different from homelessness for men and that those differences can be explained on the basis of gender. The definition of gender applied in this study is that used by Edwin M. Schur (1983) in *Labeling*

Women Deviant: "sociocultural and psychological shaping, patterning, and evaluating of female and male behavior" (p. 10).

One of the major factors that shapes and patterns behavior is the family, which historically has had a patriarchal structure. The revival of feminism and the changing sex roles for women have altered somewhat that familial structure with the advent of so many working women. The lower wage average for women, however, has retained the man as the majority wage earner. Although wives today are more involved in decision making in the family, if an agreement cannot be reached, the husband's view still predominates (Heiss, 1986). In 1981, 62% of women between 18 and 64 were workers outside the home. This would seem to indicate that the American family with two wage earners would be in good financial shape (Burnham, 1986). The stark facts are that in 1988 there were 146 divorces per 1,000 white marriages and 311 divorces per 1,000 black marriages (Statistical Abstract of the United States, 1990). Divorce, obviously, has an impact on a woman's economic situation. Noting that divorce can cause a sharp drop in a wife's income, Corcoran, Duncan, and Hill (1984) stated that, "Alimony and child support payments from an ex-husband are rare and, even if paid, usually do not represent more than a fraction of the lost income (1984, p. 241). The combination of low wage status and the high divorce rate has resulted in a high proportion of the poor being female (Burnham, 1986). A study (Bahr & Garrett, 1970) of shelter women in New York revealed that 77% had been married and that 89% of these marriages had ended in divorce, separation, annulment, or desertion, compared to 40-50% for other women. Bahr and Garrett concluded that occupational roles for women had little relevance as a cause for homelessness, but that the dissolution of marriage was "most salient" (p. 135).

Although not all homeless women are from low-income families, the majority are (Golden, 1986). A study (Irelan, 1968) by the U.S. Department of Health, Education, and Welfare revealed a distinct difference in gender roles between husband and wife in low-income families. The husband seemed to play a minimal role in the low-income family, demanding a "titular authority while at the same time demanding freedom to come and go at will" (p. 18). The man felt "dominant" and belonged to a "cult of masculine superiority" while the woman was "downtrodden," reluctant to assert herself, and thought of herself as a mother in order to compensate for the husband's lack of attention to the mother and children (pp. 19-21). Such dependency can have disastrous results. Stephanie Golden (1986), working with the homeless in New York, has stated, "Where the essence of woman is considered to be contingency and dependence, homelessness becomes a natural complement of marriage" (p. 247). When the husband leaves, the dependent woman is without financial and emotional reserves. The research of sociologist Jan L. Hagen (1986), with people who applied for shelter at Travelers Aid in Albany, New York, is significant in this regard. Hagen found that women and their children were at high risk for homelessness because of family violence and eviction, while men were more likely to become homeless due to unemployment, being released from jail, or alcohol abuse.

In 1987, single-parent, female-headed households represented 61% of all poor families with children (Statistical Abstract of the United States, 1989). Aid to Families with Dependent Children (AFDC) and food stamps comprise what the general public refers to as "welfare." These are the major programs in the United States to help female single parents (Kamerman, 1986). In 1979, 3.3 million households, or more than a third of all families headed by women, received AFDC benefits (Hopper & Hamberg, 1984). The Federal poverty level for a family of four in February 1989 was $12,000 (Welfare Advocates, 1990). The maximum monthly grant for a family of four on AFDC and food stamps in Maryland in 1990 was $477 (Welfare Advocates, 1990). AFDC is inadequate for families with no other source of income and results in a mother often choosing between food, shelter, and utilities because she can rarely pay for all three. In 1981, women constituted more than 40% of all renters (Birch, 1985). When the rent has not been paid, the family is evicted. Homelessness is often the result (Birch, 1985).

Some homeless women may possibly share another commonality besides poverty. Psychiatrist Ellen Bassuk (1986), based on hundreds of interviews with homeless mothers in Boston, found that:

> . . . some who were most chronically homeless came from homes . . . where they had lost both parents and even ended up in an institution or with a relative. Others had been abused or neglected by their own mothers. (p. 88)

In addition, the women had poor relationships with men and other women, had poor or nonexistent work histories, and many had been on welfare for 2 years or more.

A study by Stephen Crystal (1984), a sociologist in New York, focused on gender and its relationship to homelessness. He concluded that although there was little difference between homeless men and homeless women in level of education, health problems, and feelings about life in general, there were significant variations. The women were more likely to have been married previously, to have had psychiatric treatment, and to have had family difficulties in childhood. They were less likely than the men to have been in prison or to have been employed. Crystal also found that although the women might be separated from their children, they still maintained contact with them and hoped to regain custody of them, an attitude significantly different from that of homeless men. The women were also more likely than men to have married or to have an extended relationship, and 70% were in this category. Of the shelter women in Crystal's study, only 16% had reached their thirties without being hospitalized, while this was true for 26% of the men. The childhoods of the women also were more troubled than those of the men: 7.4% of the women, compared with 2.8% of the men, had grown up in foster care; and 20% of the women compared with 13.2% of the men had not lived with either parent during most of their childhood. The data also showed that women were three times more likely than men to have never been employed. Although children are not a salient factor in the lives of homeless men, 53% of the women in Crystal's research had at least one child and 76% of these women had plans to rejoin their children or saw such a reunion as a "possibility." Crystal concluded that these women clearly are not disaffiliated. He also is careful to point out that these were inhabitants of shelters and that the women who do not come into shelters might reflect different data.

More research on homeless women is needed before there is conclusive evidence that the causes, daily life patterns, and "cures" for homelessness differ for women from those of men. What data are available, nevertheless, indicate that to be homeless in America is not the same experience for women as it is for men.

DISAFFILIATION

The disaffiliation to which Crystal refers is based on the work of Gerald R. Garrett and Howard M. Bahr, who have done extensive research on disaffiliation in the lives of skid row alcoholic men (Bahr, 1973) and women in shelters in New York (Bahr & Garrett, 1976; Garrett & Bahr, 1976). Their research has shown that there are differences in disaffiliation for these two groups.

The definition of disaffiliation that Bahr (1973) has used in his work with homeless men is "a detachment from society characterized by the absence of attenuation of the affiliative bonds that link settled persons to a *network* of interconnected social structures" (emphasis mine, p. 23). Another term used by Bahr and Garrett is "unjoinedness," a condition that can be experienced by those who move from a "well-defined set of roles to a relatively undefined status" (p. 1). By contrast, affiliation exists when a person lives with someone, is employed, or voluntarily maintains membership in an association.

Garrett and Bahr (1973) found that although the ratio of male alcoholics to female alcoholics in the general population was 5 to 1, this was not true in the homeless population. There was no significant difference between the percentage of male and female alcoholics. However, men showed a larger proportion of heavy drinkers than did the women. One of the significant differences between male and female alcoholics in the study was that the women drank alone, compared to the men who drank in groups and thus were more group oriented and had more social contact than other men on skid row. The conclusion of the authors was that " . . . homeless women alcoholics may very well be the most isolated and disaffiliated residents of skid row" (p. 1240).

In addition to this work with skid row residents, Garrett and Bahr (1976) have also studied the family backgrounds of skid row women in New York. The authors tested two hypotheses: that the family backgrounds of skid row women would not differ from that of skid row men, and that women from broken homes are not overrepresented in the skid row population. The results indicated that "over half of the shelter women, compared to one third of the men, reported that they were reared in families where one or both parents were missing" (p. 378). Not only was there a significant difference in the number of broken homes, but also the causes were different because two thirds of the men reported the death of a parent as the reason for a family breakup, while the same percentage of women reported that divorce, separation, or desertion was the cause of the disruption. The authors also learned that homeless women were more likely to remarry than homeless men; infidelity and drinking were the major reasons given by women for the breakup of their own marriages; and homeless men were three times as likely to be childless as homeless women. The authors concluded that there was:

> . . . a strong link between "failures with the men in their lives" (divorce, desertion, or death) and disaffiliation and downward mobility among women, while for men disaffiliation and homelessness seem to be more closely associated with failures in occupation. (Garrett & Bahr, 1976, p. 381)

Garrett and Bahr stated that the prominence of family experience "reflects the greater priority of the roles of daughter, wife, and mother in the woman's role set" (p. 381).

Disaffiliation is an important aspect of research on homeless women. Women in the mainstream of American life develop a network of social structures and have a well-defined set of roles. American females are conditioned to be wives and mothers. Additionally, they have been expected to be members of voluntary associations such as Parent Teacher Associations, charitable organizations, and church groups. Women are held responsible for maintaining the social network within the family as well as within the neighborhood and community. Is the lack of such affiliations in the lives of homeless women an important factor in their activities, their views of themselves, and their hopes for the future?

The women in the shelters who shared soap and cigarettes with this author as well as information, were very sociable. One offered to lend me her nail polish. I stayed at the shelters at the beginning of the month when I knew the welfare checks had been received because a woman would have money for a room in a cheap hotel. For this reason, the number of women in shelters would be the lowest for the month. I also chose the month of July, when I knew the weather would not be a factor in driving women inside. I had a current driver's license in the pocket of my shirt in case I was in an accident or became ill and had to be hospitalized, but I used my maiden name with everyone I met. Psychologically I knew I was not homeless, that I had an apartment less than two miles away. Yet I ended my participation after two nights and three days because I was becoming deeply depressed. In three days, no one used my name and I began to understand how one's identity can be lost. I was simply a homeless person. I also knew that a homeless woman might need my bed.

Although this experiment in homelessness was done seven years ago, I believe that it would be difficult to replicate today. The number of homeless people has increased steadily in the intervening time, and the likelihood of a shelter having an extra empty bed at any time in 1991 is small. The experience has proven helpful in several respects. I saw the operators of the shelters as they treated the residents when no outsiders were present. I did not get a "tour" of the shelters as I might have if I had made an appointment to visit. The women whom I have interviewed since that time have often been more trustful in sharing their lifestories when they learn that I have lived as they are now living. And lastly, but most importantly, the view inside is very different from the view outside.

Spradley (1979) asked a relevant question for research with homeless women: "Ethnography for what? For understanding the human species, but also for serving the needs of humankind" (p. 16). By using an ethnographic approach, the homeless women of Baltimore are allowed to break their silence, to explain their world and to offer their solutions.

4

THE PATHS TO HOMELESSNESS

"I can't believe that this has happened to me," said a woman staying at the Salvation Army emergency shelter. Because of the lack of information on all aspects of the lives of homeless women, I was interested in what events precipitate a woman's displacement from a home into a shelter and what events in her life, if any, can predispose a woman toward homelessness. During the interviews, I asked women to describe not only their daily activities, but also their lives before they became homeless. The women were amazingly candid. Three types of homeless women participated in the interviews: those who had been institutionalized for mental illness; those who were substance abusers; and those who were situationally homeless. These broad classifications allow society to categorize the homeless into several stereotypes. One such stereotype lumps all homeless women together as "bag ladies." A second stereotype views the woman as either "deserving" or "undeserving"—the substance abusers considered as undeserving because they have "brought this situation on themselves." Another stereotype represents those who can be salvaged (the situationally homeless) and those who cannot (the bag ladies and substance abusers). Even within the classification of situationally homeless there are women such as welfare mothers who may be considered by the mainstream to be both undeserving and non-salvageable.

An ethnographic approach shows that these classifications are inadequate in describing homeless women. Within each classification there is variation and overlap. For example, although the women's backgrounds vary, there are some similarities in their paths into homelessness. Additionally, some substance abusers have spent time in mental institutions. The classifications also carry simplistic notions of both causation and "cures" for homelessness. To what extent are these classifications accurate? To what extent are the stereotypes based on these classifications true? The classifications point to real issues and serve as starting points for discussion.

THE MENTALLY ILL WOMAN IN BALTIMORE

Dorothy wore maternity clothes for 6 months, said she had the baby, but then it died. She has never been pregnant.

Elizabeth B. has tried to kill herself seven times.

Billie sees snakes and reptiles everywhere she looks.

Most people would agree that these are descriptions of women who are mentally ill. In fact, all of these women had received psychiatric treatment in mental hospitals and were considered *deinstitutionalized,* a term used to describe the mentally ill who have been released from institutional care. There has been controversy over the number of homeless who are mentally ill. Projections have ranged from 10% (Snow, Baker, & Anderson, 1986) to 90% (Bassuk, Rubin, & Lauriat, 1984).

An additional problem in determining the actual percentage of mentally ill homeless is that it is not always easy to determine if an observed disorder is the cause of being homeless or a consequence (Cuomo, 1983). Studies such as that of Salerno, Hopper, and Baxter (1984) and Baxter and Hopper (1981) have described the disorientation and confusion that can result from the anxieties of living in the world of uncertainty populated by the homeless. One study in Baltimore (Breakey & Fischer, 1985) stated that most mental hospitals discourage in-patient treatment.

Consequently, many of the younger mentally ill homeless may not have received any psychiatric care. In Maryland the Governor's Advisory Board Report separated mental health, mental retardation, and substance abuse into three categories. For Baltimore, the report identified the following percentages in the area of special needs for those seeking shelter during fiscal year 1985: "Mental health, 27%; Mental retardation, 5%; Substance abuse, 38%" (Maryland Department of Human Resources, 1986, p. 146). If all three of these special needs were grouped under the category of mental illness, the total of mentally ill for Baltimore would be 70%.

Bag ladies constitute the principal number of homeless according to the mainstream stereotype. Certainly some of the women who live in the streets are part of the classification of mentally ill women. Urban dwellers have seen the disheveled woman standing on the corner raving at invisible foes, eating out of garbage dumpsters, and sleeping in a doorway surrounded by her shopping bags. Yet it is difficult to determine if all of these women are mentally ill. Appearances and behaviors may be due to other factors. Baxter and Hopper

(1981), based on studies of the homeless in New York City, have pointed out that the unwashed body and unbrushed teeth of a woman can act sometimes to discourage men's interests and additionally that these women often have a fear of strangers. Consequently, it has been difficult to research and evaluate the mental health of these women. My study includes women called "bag ladies," who until 1986-1987 lived in the streets and, because of an outreach program run by Catholic Charities, have availed themselves of the services of the Park Avenue Lodge. This lodge offers year-long shelter to women who were not accepted at the other shelters in Baltimore because of their erratic and sometimes violent behavior.

No women living in the streets were interviewed formally or in-depth for this study, although several were observed and interviewed informally. One woman who fit the description of a bag lady was Adele, a drunk and disturbed woman who came to the Salvation Army canteen truck one night. She could hardly stand up and she spit on and threw pennies and quarters at passersby. It was obvious that she needed help. I spent 45 minutes talking to her, trying to keep her from creating a row with other patrons of "the block," and trying to prevent her from leaving. Another volunteer had called the police, and I waited for the 911 patrol car. We hoped that we could convince the police that she was dangerous to others and herself, for without someone to explain to others that she was sick, she could have been assaulted for the punches she threw at any man who came within striking distance. She showed me her empty bottle of Thunderbird, but she also mentioned that she had been in a hospital five times and that "they tried to kill me." She said that her son had been killed in Vietnam, and that she had an 87-year-old father living in South Carolina. Periodically she pulled up her sweater, encrusted with dirt, and tried to expose her breasts. When I would pull her sweater down and try to calm her, she would start to cry and try to kiss my hand while saying "Yes, ma'am" repeatedly. The kerchief came off her hair to reveal a gray haired woman, possibly in her fifties, with most of her teeth missing. She was also blind in one eye. Her black skin was covered with dirt, and her feet were shod in large men's tennis shoes. She needed help, but she did not seem to want it. When one of the volunteers mentioned that she could go to a hospital, she pulled away, raced across the street, and disappeared around a corner. The patrol car never answered the call. As a woman who works with At Jacob's Well, an outreach program for the homeless, told me, "There are women out there who have no contact with anyone, and they want it to stay that way."

This outreach worker's conclusion may have no validity, for no one can say with authority if the women "want it to stay that way." These women are in a terrible situation and whatever their mental conditions, their behavior indicates that they feel threatened and frightened. They may very well *want* help, but some may be incapable of articulating that desire.

Adele.

Some women discharged from mental hospitals return to their families and may never become homeless. For others, however, the support system that they need in order to remain deinstitutionalized is not there because of a severe shortage of community health programs. After being discharged, many homeless find themselves in the streets. One woman told me that when she was discharged from one of the state hospitals in Maryland, she was given bus fare to downtown Baltimore and a two-week supply of her medication.

In a study of the mentally ill in Boston by Bassuk, Rubin, and Lauriat (1984), the authors stated that their data supported the likely hypothesis that the homeless mentally ill are "more disconnected from support networks than are those with a home" (p. 1,549), based on data that 74% of shelter residents had no family relationships and 73% had no friends. The women I interviewed who admitted to being hospitalized for mental illness also acknowledged the stress between them and their families. Thus when discharged from the hospital, either the woman chose not to return to her family or the family did not want her to return. The women had arrived at mental hospitals by various routes. However, they had arrived at shelters by the same route because after they were released by the hospitals, they had nowhere else to go. Family and friends were no longer able or willing to help, and some women did not want to return to their families because the conflicts that aggravated their illnesses had not been resolved. Yvonne, a woman at Upton House who had been institutionalized several times, told me, "I write letters to my mother, but I'm not ready to deal with her." Desiree, of Marian House, who also had spent several periods of time in mental hospitals said, "My sister put me in the hospital. I'm not going to stay with her." Coping with the stresses and problems of modern American urban life without someone to help has proved overwhelming for these women. They have been fortunate, however, to find shelters with a different kind of support system than that of a family, and they are not living in the streets as bag ladies.

Nine of the 22 women I interviewed had been previously hospitalized for mental illness, eight of them more than once. Two of them had been arrested and were sent to mental hospitals from jail, another had been sent by a half-way house in which she was staying, and another had been sent from a detoxification center. Two women had been sent by family members. The shortest stay in a mental hospital had been 2 1/2 months and the longest had been 10 1/2 months. Of the nine women who had been hospitalized for mental illness, three had been abused as children by their fathers and one had been abused by her husband. Six of the women said they had been "depressed," wanted to kill themselves, or wanted to sleep all the time. Depressive disorders are one of the main diagnoses for women in all types of treatment facilities (Wilson, 1986). One woman had had her child placed in foster care because she had abused her son through neglect: she did not leave her apartment for days and did not feed the child or herself.

The majority of women who had been hospitalized were on medication such as lithium, which is prescribed for manic depression, and/or seeing a psychiatrist when I interviewed them. Most of the women were clean and neatly dressed. When I talked with them they were lucid and rational and none of them fantasized. These homeless women are examples of those who did not fit the stereotypes of hopeless bag ladies, although several of them have lived in the streets.

Some of the former bag ladies have taken advantage of the Park Avenue Lodge. One of the guests was Dorothy, a woman I had met four years earlier at My Sister's Place (MSP). At that time she scowled at everyone, answered in monosyllables, and rushed across the room as if in a fury. Yet her voice was so low as to be almost inaudible. During that year she began to wear maternity clothes and told people that Tom, the Catholic layworker at MSP, was the father. Dorothy is in her early forties and Tom was 22. Later, she told people that she had the baby, but that it had died. A short time after that she was arrested for stealing tools from a transit bus. She then was sent back to Springfield State Hospital. Her life during the next few years was a series of stays in cheap hotels and emergency shelters interspersed with admissions to the state hospital. In the fall of 1987 she came to the Park Avenue Lodge. The woman I saw there smiled, chatted with me, and played a board game with another woman and me. At the time, Dorothy was not ready to function on her own—she may never be. Yet at the Park Avenue Lodge she could live in a group situation when four years before she did not associate with anyone, could smile and chat, and could move at a moderate pace rather than the furious racing that marked her movements before.

Yvonne was another deinstitutionalized woman who had lived in the streets. After being released from a state hospital in the early 1980s, she lived in shelters and ate in soup kitchens in Washington, DC. Travelers Aid sent her to Baltimore, which is where she had lived before her hospitalization. She lived from April to December in the streets of Baltimore before she was arrested for trespassing and sent back to Springfield State Hospital for five months. She then spent an additional four months in the Walter P. Carter Psychiatric Center of University Hospital in Baltimore. She was living in a house supported by the Woman's Housing Coalition and seeing a psychiatrist when I interviewed her in August 1986. She was able to live successfully in a group house and was making steps toward living independently.

For some women a double burden of mental illness and substance abuse has resulted in their displacement from permanent housing, either with family or alone. Lily's story of how and why she came to be living at Marian House is an example of some of the women whom I interviewed who have had mental problems as well as problems with substance abuse. Lily's mother was divorced when Lily was young and she lived with her mother until she herself married. Born in rural Maryland, she moved to Virginia with her husband. After the birth of her son when she was 23, her husband became abusive and although she wanted to leave, she stayed for the sake of her child and because she "felt sorry" for her husband. She worked as a security guard at night and began to use cocaine and alcohol to escape her problems. She asked her husband to get help for their troubled marriage, but he said that they did not need outsiders. She told me,

> *He was jealous—of my family, the baby, my job. When the baby was six months old I had to call the cops on him. He drank a lot and he came home drunk this day and beat me and went through the house. He once held a knife to the baby's throat.*

Finally, she tried to kill her husband. She took a 357 magnum and aimed the gun at him, but she "thought of the baby" and she put the gun down. In July 1986, her husband agreed that she needed to get away, perhaps to a girlfriend's house. Instead, she took the car and drove to Maryland, leaving her 3-year-old behind. Lily did not take the baby with her because she was afraid that she would hurt him. When I interviewed her she had seen her son only once since that July; when her husband realized that she was not coming back, he refused to let her see the child again. She spent a week and a half at a truck stop before she finally called her father, who agreed to take her in even though he had remarried and had three other children. Her mother had Lily's brother and sister-in-law living with her and had no room. While staying at her father's, she went to the county mental health facility where she was put on tranquilizers. She "got strung out on those" and took a half a bottle one day. She awoke in the county hospital and was then admitted to Springfield State Hospital, where she remained for three months. In February 1987, she left the state hospital and was accepted by Marian House, a transitional house for the homeless. Although she did not know where she would go when she left the shelter, she was hopeful that Marian House would give her the help she needed to live independently. Marian House might indeed have helped her, for as Wolins and Wozner (1977) said about deinstitutionalization, "People are made into healthy humans by their interaction with a competent social environment" (p. 605).

In addition to a "competent social environment," appropriate medication, and continued psychiatric treatment, some homeless women have found another incentive for regaining their mental health. One such woman I observed in a transitional house was the mother of three children, aged 10, 8, and 6, who were living with her parents in a Southern state. (This was the woman mentioned previously who hallucinated and saw reptiles and snakes.) More than anything else she wanted to have her children with her, but her mental problems were so overpowering that she could only have her children visit her for short periods of time. The resident director at the shelter was convinced that this woman's desire to reclaim her children would eventually help her to become well enough to realize her wish.

Some women have not been able to gain sufficient control of their lives to enable them to live independently. They have entered a cycle of hospital to shelter to hospital that can be very difficult to break. With assistance, however, many other deinstitutionalized women in Baltimore could permanently escape homelessness.

FEMALE SUBSTANCE ABUSERS IN BALTIMORE

Helen, the alcoholic companion of the central character in William Kennedy's *Ironweed* (1983), was called a "drunk and a whore" (p. 136) by male drunks. In *Gone With the Wind,* Scarlett gargled with cologne so that Rhett would not know she had been drinking. The association of shame and alcohol helps explain the secrecy with which many women in this country have used alcohol, and the difficulty in determining the number of female alcoholics in the general population, as well as the number of homeless female alcoholics. Many women refuse to seek help because of the general public's attitude toward female drunkenness. Female alcoholics sometimes have ended up on skid rows, although the skid rows of the past were often dominated by alcoholic men, and alcoholic women were a minority (Garrett and Bahr, 1973). Today it is not uncommon to find homeless female substance abusers who are doubly addicted to alcohol and drugs. Of the 11 women interviewed who were substance abusers, 7 admitted to being "addicted" to both alcohol and drugs.

One of the mainstream stereotypes of homeless women is that many of them are alcoholics or drug abusers. The reasoning of the mainstream is, "Their drinking or drug use is their own choice. If they wanted to quit they could, but they don't want to. They are worthless and undeserving of help. They like living the way that they do." Although substance abuse does play a role in the lives of some homeless women, the majority of these women are not the fictional Helen of *Ironweed,* who traveled with an alcoholic tramp and lived the life of a derelict.

Some women, however, have not been able to escape their alcoholism permanently. Henrietta agreed to talk to me one day when I was visiting My Sister's Place. At 51, her lined face and lack of upper teeth made her look many years older. Divorced six years earlier, she had seen neither her grown son nor daughter for three years and did not know where they were. Henrietta worked for 29 years until six years before the interview when she was struck by a car. The accident forced her to spend months in a hospital. She did not remember the accident that hospitalized her, but said that she had not been drinking. For the three years before our meeting she had lived with friends here and there. Because she had moved around so much, she had lost "all of her things and court papers." She qualified for Social Security Disability Insurance (SSDI) because she is 85% disabled. She explained her situation in trying to live on $300 a month:

> *I stayed where I could on three hundred a month. Sometimes I rented a room; other times I had no place and slept in vacant houses. When I didn't have no money to buy food, I've eaten out of dumpsters behind restaurants. Even an animal do that—so will people to survive. I ate at soup kitchens and I ended up sleeping in parks and empty cars and stuff.*

When I interviewed Henrietta, she had recently been released from the seven-day detox at South Baltimore General Hospital. She told me that ''they'' wanted her to go to the 28-day detox program at University Hospital. She had two epileptic seizures from drinking and also had an ulcer and a ''hianus hernia'' [hiatal hernia]. Henrietta was staying at the Salvation Army emergency shelter but had no idea where she would go after she used her allotted 21 days.

Salvation Army admissions office.

Lydia was another example of a woman who had made attempts to overcome her alcoholism, but had not been successful. I first saw Lydia at the Salvation Army shelter when I had gone there with the Coordinator of Residential Housing for the Woman's Housing Coalition who was to interview and select one of two women for a vacancy at Upton House. Lydia was the one who was accepted, mainly because the other woman had severe mental problems and would have required more attention than the staff at Upton House could provide. Lydia had come to the Salvation Army from a detoxification unit. When I next saw Lydia, she had settled into Upton House and was acclimating herself. In her interview with the coordinator she said, "I get involved with a lot of men when I drink. I don't do that when I'm sober." From the time she came to Upton House and during the next seven months, Lydia went to Alcoholics Anonymous (AA) meetings and got a job working as a cleaning lady. Born in Kentucky, she had not graduated from high school and had been married and divorced.

I requested an in-depth interview with her on several occasions, but she always put me off. According to her answers on the questionnaire, she had never worked longer than six months at a job, had spent her childhood with a mother and stepfather, was living in a shelter for the first time, and had become homeless because of domestic problems. One of the other residents who became friendly with her told me that she had been asked to leave her daughter's home because of her drinking. Lydia also answered that she had been in jail, a mental hospital, and had lived on the streets.

In the fall of 1986, a local artist taught an art class to the residents of the Women's Housing Coalition's transitional shelters. Lydia attended often. She had a "very strong sense of design and an almost Van Gogh type of primitive quality to her work," according to the teacher. During this time she did not drink because she was attending AA meetings regularly. By late December, she was very excited that she had been able to buy her grandson a new coat and some toys for Christmas with the salary she had earned as a cleaning lady. She spent Christmas with her daughter, son-in-law, and grandson and had "a wonderful time." Shortly after that she stopped attending AA meetings. In February, after leaving her therapist's office at a local hospital, she fell stepping off a curb and broke her leg. Although always very thin, she had gained some weight while staying at Upton House and had made herself more attractive by styling her hair and wearing makeup. After her fall, she seemed to lose interest in her appearance. A resident at Upton House told me that the doctor had given Lydia some kind of medication for the pain and she was taking the pills all of the time. Lydia had told me that once she had been addicted to pills and alcohol. While she was recovering from her broken leg, she lost her job. Several weeks after the cast was removed, Lydia left Upton House. The police later reported to the coordinator that she was again in a detoxification unit. She walked out of the detox unit, was later arrested for being drunk and disorderly, spent 30 days in jail, and upon her release, met a male alcoholic and moved in with him. She did not return to Upton House.

Erlena exemplified the teenage alcoholic who functioned within a family setting until alcohol controlled her and she left home. At 32, Erlena had faced an intent-to-murder charge and the possibility of 20 years in prison. She admitted that her drinking was to blame. Erlena's mother never married her father. The stepfather Erlena acquired at the age of five was an alcoholic who rarely brought his paychecks home. When she was 14, Erlena got a job and continued to go to school. She began to drink at lunchtime. At age 15 she moved in with her grandmother and continued to drink whenever she could. When her grandmother went into a senior citizens' home, Erlena went back to her mother's home. After graduating from high school, she joined the U.S. Army. Erlena played basketball for the Army and became a weapons specialist. While she was in the Army, she would "drink, black out, rob somebody, and get violent." Afraid that she might go to jail, she got a discharge. She never kept a job for more than six months after that, and when she was fired from her last job in 1985, she again moved back home.

Erlena's stepfather had been sober for six years when she moved back home. He "aggravated and harrassed" her and one day called the police to have her removed. While she was using the telephone to call her sister, he wrapped the cord of the phone around her neck. She got a knife from a nearby drawer and stabbed him, "twice in the chest and in his intestines." He lived to press charges against her. Erlena spent six months in jail because no one would raise bail for her. Several women from New Directions for Women came to the jail, and Erlena wrote the director a letter explaining her background. The director arranged for Erlena to be put on five years probation under the supervision of the director. Then Erlena qualified to enter the Bradley Center, which helps vets get jobs. She was a printer trainee and living at Marian House when I interviewed her. She attended AA meetings regularly.

Pam, a 29-year-old single woman who was staying at Marian House, was another example of a substance abuser who became addicted as a teenager. One of seven children of an alcoholic mother, she was beaten with pipes, a belt, and her mother's fists. Quitting school after the eighth grade, Pam began to drink and take drugs to "get in with the crowd." She worked, stole from her mother, or "tricked" in order to get money. Her life from ages 19 to 27 was series of living with different friends and then moving back home until the next incident with her family sent her away. She finally got a job at a "carburetor place" but didn't pay her mother her rent and was put out of the house. She was a heroin addict who "was living for the drug."

For the next two years Pam lived in storage and laundry rooms and slept on park benches and in condemned houses, primarily in the area of Pennsylvania Avenue in Baltimore where the "shooting galleries" (abandoned houses used by heroin addicts) are. When she finally went to the Department of Social Services

(DSS) for help, she weighed 90 pounds, stood 5′ 8″, and suffered from malnutrition. DSS sent her to the Karis Hospice, which then sent her to Marian House, where she was trying to put her life together. Ironically, although she used both drugs and alcohol for a period of time, she primarily used drugs because she "didn't want to drink and be like my mother." While at Marian House she began to attend Narcotics Anonymous (NA) meetings.

Cookie, at 18, was the youngest homeless woman I interviewed. She too was a doubly-addicted substance abuser. Cookie's father was in the U.S. Army and her mother died when Cookie was 13. She went to live with an aunt for the next few years. When she left her aunt's she went to Florida. She told me that because she was using drugs and alcohol and became careless with contraception, she became pregnant. She wouldn't have an abortion. "I just couldn't," she said. After the birth, she put the baby up for adoption and came back to Baltimore. Rather than live with her family, she got a job as a nanny and took care of a nine-year-old girl whose parents were living out of state. She lost her job because of drinking and went to the shelter in Laurel, MD, where she took an overdose. She "went to the psych ward" for 17 days and then went to Antioch House for three days before coming to Marian House. She had recently contacted her father and she was attending seven AA meetings a week. She had been diagnosed as manic depressive and took medication for the condition. Cookie had left high school several months before she was to graduate, but while at Marian House she was studying for her General Equivalency Diploma (GED).

Other women have become substance abusers later in life. One such woman, who had a successful career and then lost it because of drugs, was Myla. She had been a teacher in the Baltimore city-school system for nine and a half years. She separated from her husband and met a man who used drugs and who introduced her to them. It is important in Myla's story to know that she was a large woman, with huge hips and legs, and believed that she was not attractive. But she had a striking and handsome face and a well-articulated and resonant voice. The man she loved and lived with was arrested for dealing drugs and was sent to jail, but was released on early parole. Thirteen days after he came home to her, he died of a drug overdose. Myla said, "I thought my world was over." By this time she had lost her job, her career, and her house. Shortly after that she became involved with another man who also used drugs and alcohol as did she. During the next three years, she moved 11 times. She had spent time in jail and had lived with friends for several years. She was arrested for a "bank scam" and was sentenced to 90 days. Upon her release she was sent to Hollins Place, a treatment center, and then went into long-term treatment. She was living at Marian House, hoping to fight her way back. Because of her criminal record, a return to public school teaching was doubtful. But she was striving to be drug free and self-supporting.

The majority of women were looking for help and were trying to become drug free. Although addiction is a life-long problem, by participating in either Alcoholics Anonymous or Narcotics Anonymous or both, and living in a supportive and secure environment, many of the homeless women who are substance abusers could begin their return to the mainstream.

THE SITUATIONALLY HOMELESS WOMAN IN BALTIMORE

The major cause of women being situationally homeless in America today is their poverty. When two out of three poor adults in the United States today are women, it is not surprising that women are living in the streets or in shelters (Lefkowitz & Withorn, 1986). In ancient Israel a man was valued at 50 shekels and a woman at 30 shekels; in modern America a woman is paid 66 cents for every dollar that a man earns (Wallis, 1989). A woman who has lost her job and cannot find another, a woman who has been abused by her husband or family, or a woman whose husband has abandoned her: all of these women can be situationally homeless, for without money, they have no resources but the shelters or the streets.

This is the group of homeless women that the mainstream finds the most deserving. Within this group, however, may be found the woman who has had her Aid to Families with Dependent Children (AFDC) payment cut, or the General Public Assistance (GPA) recipient who chose to eat instead of paying for her room in a cheap hotel. These are the so-called ''welfare cheats''—those who ''live off of the rest of us, who could work, but won't,'' as many Americans believe. The women who were situationally homeless were *all* receiving some form of public assistance or accepting charity. Even the few who had found jobs were living in housing supported by charitable organizations at the time of these interviews.

Some of the situationally homeless women had been victims of abuse. Ann, who was abused by her family, lived at Upton House, a transitional shelter, for more than a year. She was ready to move into a place of her own, but ''Section 8's'' (federal rent subsidies) are difficult to obtain. Ann had been married for a short time many years ago. Later she moved in with her parents and brothers and sisters. She collected Supplemental Security Income (SSI) because she had many physical problems and could not work. She came to Upton House because her sister hit her when Ann asked for $100 of her monthly SSI check and as a result of the blow, Ann ended up in the hospital. When she left the hospital, although she had no money and nowhere to go, she refused to return to her mother's home.

Other women may be homeless because they have recently been released from jail. Fay was one such woman. One of five children born to an alcoholic mother and a truck driver, her father sexually abused her from age 3 to 14. Fay was ''born without eardrums'' as was her brother. She spent a great deal of her childhood in hospitals and learned to lip read and to use gestures. In school she was considered retarded and her "math is still on a first-grade level." She "thought about suicide all the time" when she was a child. She married at 20 and had a child. She and her husband fought constantly, and her five-year-old daughter suffers from gastroenteritis. Fay left her daughter with her husband because he can "provide better for her" financially, although he abused Fay and that is why she left. She lived in and out of shelters after she left as well as camped in a woods in the suburbs while she worked at a movie theater. She married her husband because she was pregnant, and her "mother couldn't afford her and the baby." Several months before I interviewed her, she was arrested for vandalism. After serving some time in jail, she went to Marian House. She did not wish to live with friends, and she had no money for a place of her own.

In addition to the other causes of situational homelessness, inability to pay the rent because of the small amount a woman receives from welfare is common. Eileen, for example, was the mother of six children, the oldest 24 and the youngest 16. The 16-year-old and her 18-year-old sister were both pregnant when I met Eileen. Neither was married. The 18-year-old also had a two-year-old son who was in foster care. While at Upton House Eileen got a job as a night guard at one of the city's public housing projects. She had grown up in poverty, and had left school somewhere around the eighth grade. She was pregnant at age 15. Because her former husband had never paid child support since the breakup of her marriage 15 years earlier, Eileen had lived on welfare and had also worked in a small grocery store earning $70–$80 a week. Her last apartment before Upton House was one she shared with her youngest daughter, but her welfare payment could not cover both rent and utilities. Because she was late with the rent month after month, the landlord finally evicted her. She found the Woman's Housing Coalition in the yellow pages of the phone book. After a six-month stay at Upton House, she once more moved into her own apartment.

Women can become homeless for other reasons. One woman I interviewed was widowed at age 27. She became ill and when she was released from the hospital, she had no one to take her in. Another woman had come from New York and had been mugged and robbed. When she went to the police, they sent her to My Sister's Place, who in turn sent her to Upton House. A woman from the eastern shore of Maryland came to Baltimore to get work; when she ran out of money, she ended up in a shelter.

The common denominator for all of these women is lack of money for shelter and food. Barbara Ehrenreich (1986) believes that rising divorce rates and increasing numbers of childbirths occurring out of wedlock have resulted in women having the principal responsibility for supporting themselves and their children. She also stated that, "At the same time, most women remain locked into dead-end jobs with wages too low to support themselves, let alone sustain a

TABLE 1 Percentages of types of homeless women

Type	Interviewees ($N = 22$)	Questionnaire ($N = 89$)
Mentally ill	40.9%	24.7%
Situational	50%	73%
Substance abuse	50%[a]	0%[b]

[a]Substance abuse for some women preceded stays in mental hospitals. Although 11 of the women revealed in interviews that they were substance abusers, 9 of those had spent time in mental hospitals.

[b]The questionnaire did not include a question asking women to report on substance abuse.

family'' (p. 20). Poverty and women are so closely associated in the United States that Diana Pearce (1978) has coined the term "the feminization of poverty'' (p. 28). Whatever the immediate cause of a woman's homelessness or why she finds herself living in a shelter, it is her lack of money that forces her to be a homeless woman.

The ultimate cause of homelessness for a woman may indeed be mental illness, alcoholism, drug addiction, or an emergency situation. The precipitating cause may have been non-payment of rent, arrest for a crime, release from a mental hospital, or a multitude of other events that caused the woman to lose permanent shelter. How do these causes of female homelessness compare with the causes of male homelessness? Hopper's, Baxter's, Cox's, and Klein's (1982) survey of studies of five New York City shelters found 50–70% of the men showed some psychiatric problems and nearly 25% showed some evidence of alcohol dependency on clinical examination. No data was given on the men who were drug dependent or situationally homeless.

Table 1 shows the percentages of the three types of homeless women based on their self-reporting.

The percentages for the interviewed women who have been hospitalized are comparable to the figures for the men in Hopper et al.'s survey (1982). The women, however, have a higher percentage of substance abuse, but this figure includes both alcohol and drug abuse.

The "cause'' of a person's homelessness is a complex series of events that span the person's lifetime. Even the precipitating cause may not be correctly identified by the homeless person. For example, eviction may be reported as the cause when in reality, the person's alcoholic behavior caused the landlord to evict. Why some people become homeless and others in similar situations do not has not yet been determined. To categorize homeless women according to arbitrary classifications may be convenient for those who wish to speak of the homeless in broad terms. Individual cases, however, indicate that the women shift from one classification to another or may fit all three classifications—the mentally ill, substance abusers and the situationally homeless—at the same time. Whatever the "type" of homeless woman she may be or whatever events lead to her displacement, once a woman is on the streets, she is presented with a situation for which society has not prepared her.

5

DAILY LIFE

When Henrietta was asked, "How did you learn how to be a homeless woman?," her reply was, "I learned like a kid growing up—the best way I could. Nobody showed me the ropes." When Ada was asked the same question, she replied, "The girls who stay with you in the missions help you." When a woman first becomes homeless, she is faced with an array of problems. Where will she sleep? Where will she get food? Where can she bathe and wash her clothes? What patterns of behavior of homeless women can be observed, and how are these similar to or different from those of homeless men?

SHELTER

When a woman is displaced from her home, she must find shelter immediately or face the prospect of sleeping in the streets. The majority of women in Baltimore are referred to emergency shelters by other agencies such as My Sister's Place (MSP), Traveler's Aid, the Department of Social Services, the state mental hospitals, the police, detox units, and prison authorities. Some women may be directed to the emergency shelters by other homeless women whom they meet in soup kitchens. None of the women I interviewed found shelter this way, although I overheard a woman at My Sister's Place state that this was how she found Karis Hospice. This was not the pattern for the majority, however, who had found shelter through an agency of some kind.

My Sister's Place serves as a referral center. Once a woman visits this daytime shelter, the staff will locate a bed for her for the night or, if necessary, pay for a hotel room until shelter is available. MSP sends women to the Salvation Army shelter, the YWCA, or Karis Hospice, all of which provide emergency shelter, as well as to several other shelters. The length of stay varies from shelter to shelter.

Even referral to a shelter does not mean that a woman automatically has a place to stay. Some women who have caused problems while staying at the shelters are asked to leave. Subsequently they may not be admitted at all. One woman was refused admittance at a shelter because she had once kicked a girl, another because she had a drinking problem, and another, who was obviously mentally ill, for an unspecified reason. A woman may be asked to leave after she is admitted if her behavior does not conform to the rules. For example, during the year I visited Upton House, four women were asked to leave for returning to the house drunk. Once a woman's time in an emergency shelter is up, she will either move to a transitional shelter with the help of the staff, find her own lodgings, or move into the streets. On one occasion when the Salvation Army announced it was closing for a week for cleaning and repairs, the women, who knew they had less than a week before the shelter closed, were baffled and frightened about the uncertainty of where they would go. Some of these women had children, and there are few shelters in Baltimore that will take mothers with children. The staff at the Salvation Army Shelter helped all of the women to find shelter.

One determinant of daily life for homeless women in Baltimore is the kind of shelter in which the women are staying. The Greater Baltimore Shelter Network (GBSN) defines three kinds of sleeping facilities:

1. Night shelters generally offer safe secure sleeping facilities; some offer evening and morning meals; some have counseling and referral.
2. Twenty-four hour emergency shelters offer safe, secure sleeping facilities, three meals, showers, supervision, counseling, and referral; length of stay varies from 3 days to 8 weeks.
3. Transitional shelters generally offer safe and secure sleeping facilities and three meals (Greater Baltimore Shelter Network, 1985, p. 9).

The Karis Hospice, an example of a night shelter, is located in a very poor neighborhood that is bordered by warehouses and housing projects. The Hospice was founded in 1980 by the Women's Division of the Baltimore Rescue Mission. It is supported by churches and gifts from individuals. The hospice receives no government funding, but it is a designated recipient of United Way and receives a small portion of its funding through this organization. The primary purpose of this shelter is to lead women to Jesus Christ. This is clearly stated in the opening paragraph of the Guidelines (see Appendix 3):

Welcome! We the staff, sincerely believe that all who enter our doors come by God's providential leading in their lives, not by "chance" or "bad luck." We believe all come for a greater purpose than shelter, food, and clothing. What is that "greater" purpose? To hear about the love, grace, and mercy of God revealed to all through His Son, Jesus Christ.

This shelter, housing 15 women, is located near the heart of downtown Baltimore. Karis Hospice is located on the second floor of the Baltimore Rescue Mission, a night shelter that has beds for 150 men. The women enter the hospice by a separate door from that to the men's shelter. Women must enter the shelter by 5:00 p.m., after which time no one is admitted.

The women's shelter consists of a large classroom, a dorm with an adjoining bathroom, a breezeway (a Plexiglass-enclosed walkway between two buildings over the roof of the men's mission), and a lounge/dining room at the other end of the breezeway. The furniture is second-hand, and the rooms are kept clean because the women are assigned chores, such as vacuuming and dusting, after they have eaten their evening meal. In this way the mission is kept clean, and the women are given responsibilities to carry out. There are five iron bunkbeds in the dorm room, and there is also a separate room for one mother and her child(ren). Two meals are served each day, breakfast at 7:00 a.m. and dinner at approximately 5:15-5:45 p.m. Bible study is held after breakfast and dinner. The women are expected to attend. Women must leave the shelter after breakfast and may not return until 4:00 p.m. A woman is allowed to keep her possessions in a locker, as along as she is a guest at the shelter, a period not to exceed two weeks. The homeless women of Baltimore call this shelter "the mission." There is no charge for services.

The Karis Hospice is one of the shelters in which I stayed while documenting the lives of area homeless women. The director stated to me when she was interviewing me for admission that her first responsibility was to "bring Jesus Christ into your life and to care for your soul. If you have that, the other things will follow." She also explained to me how long I might stay and the rules. When I asked if the hospice would help me to find a job or help me to apply for welfare, the director said, "No. If you turn to God, you will find the way to solve your problems."

The rules and regulations reflect the religious nature of the mission, and the daily routine is very structured. The women enter the mission between 4 and 5 p.m. each day. Meals are at specified times, and chores are assigned and scheduled. A new guest is excused from chores on the first evening because the director interviews her at that time. The director examines a new guest's handbag for "drugs, alcohol, or pornographic materials." She asks how the woman became homeless, and then explains the rules of the mission.

After the chores are finished, there is an hour and a half mandatory Bible study, after which the women are allowed free time until lights out at 10:00 p.m. Even smoking is regulated as to time and place, allowed for only 15 minutes after dinner and for 15 minutes before bed, but only in the breezeway. If a woman leaves the building anytime before 6:00 a.m. the next morning, she may not return until the next evening at 4:00. Women are not to fraternize with the men in the Baltimore Rescue Mission downstairs (a husband may be staying downstairs and a wife upstairs, but they must wait until they are off the premises before speaking with each other). One guest at the mission commented that her husband was downstairs, but they could only see each other during the day after they left their respective shelters.

The room in which the women sleep is a communal room; each woman is assigned one of five bunkbeds for a total of ten guests. Towels and washcloths are provided, and if a woman does not have a nightgown, she is given a slip to sleep in. Nudity is discouraged. The women are allowed to take showers and chat during the time after Bible study, and a night attendant comes on duty at 10:00. Breakfast is served at 7:00 a.m., followed by a 30-minute Bible study. By 8:00 a.m. all of the women are out of the shelter.

This system of rules at Karis Hospice affects the lives of the guests in numerous ways. Some women have been grateful that there is a clean, safe place to stay. One woman said, "They are nicer to me than the Salvation Army but there aren't enough bathrooms or privacy." Another woman told me that it is "nice because they are small." Yet others have expressed resentment at the mandatory Bible study. One woman said, "If you eat their meals, you have to go to their Bible studies." Another said, "You have to go to gospel meetings or they put you out." This resentment causes some women to seek other shelter. Because a woman must tell the staff if she plans to return that evening, if she should leave without such notification and then later change her mind the bed may no longer be available. If she cannot find another bed, she may have to sleep in the streets.

Additionally, putting the women out on the street before My Sister's Place opens can be dangerous in the dark morning hours of winter. There is some sort of cruel irony in providing food and shelter for women and then forcing them to live in the streets for 10–12 hours a day. The rule requiring the women to leave in the morning enables the staff to restock supplies, do laundry, and thoroughly clean the shelter, but it also treats the women in an institutional manner. The fact that this is not their home is painfully emphasized. Cleanliness and expediency seem to have equal importance with what the women feel are more important human needs.

Also, the rule that no one may return to the shelter before 4:00 p.m. forces women to seek less desirable shelter during the day, such as on public benches where they are exposed to the weather, or in "greasy spoons" in which they may be harrassed by male vagrants. Karis Hospice also requires the women to take their belongings with them each day if they have determined in the morning that they will not return that night. Anyone who has carried plastic shopping bags filled with groceries knows the physical discomfort that can occur when carrying such parcels even a few blocks, much less for miles as one travels between soup kitchens and shelters. It seems that women who are more religiously-oriented seem to be comfortable with the rules at the mission, while others may stay there only because there is no place else to go.

An alternative to the mission is the Eleanor D. Corner House, a 24-hour emergency shelter on the fifth and sixth floors of the YWCA building located in the central business district of Baltimore. Nationally, the YWCA has a 100-year history of providing low cost shelter to women. The Women's Housing Coalition lobbied the Maryland state legislature in 1979 for funding to create a model shelter. In 1981 the Corner House was opened at the YWCA, which runs and manages the shelter with public funds.

When a woman is first admitted to the Corner House, she is allowed to stay three days, after which time she is interviewed by a counselor. If the woman signs a service plan she may stay for a maximum of eight weeks. The service plan requires the woman to set goals such as finding a job or locating housing and then to work, with the help of the staff, toward reaching those goals.

A single woman will occupy an individual bedroom, which contains a bed, dresser, chairs, lamp, and a closet. Linens are provided, and each resident also receives a bag containing soap, shampoo, toothpaste, comb, and razor. Each woman is given the key to her room that must be turned in to the floor counselor each time the guest leaves the building. Laundry facilities are available as well as a sewing machine, an iron, and ironing board. Three meals a day are served. Services are free if the woman has no income of any kind.

The YWCA also has an extensive list of rules, although the structure is less rigid. There are no religious services to attend. Women are not forced to leave the shelter during the day, although they are encouraged to find more permanent shelter and to seek employment if they sign a service plan. The YWCA allows women to stay out until midnight if they choose. There is a television in the lounge, although it may not be used until 4:30 in the afternoon. Visitors are allowed only on the first floor. For these reasons, two women who were talking at MSP one day and had stayed at the YWCA said that they liked it, but women who had been dismissed for infractions of the rules were naturally very negative.

If a homeless woman has a child or children, she will stay on a different floor than those who are alone. Laundry facilities are available also, and these families eat their meals with the single women. Similar rules apply to both groups of women, although the women with children are allowed to stay only 30 days (see Appendix 4).

The YWCA is the second shelter at which I stayed. The counselor who first interviewed me was polite but business-like. She was not unfriendly, but she never called me by name. When I reported to the dining room on the following morning at 7:30 as the guidelines stated, I found no one there. I returned to a large foyer near the elevator and sat in a chair, reading a magazine and waiting for the dining room to open. A few minutes later, a large woman stepped off the elevator and demanded to know what I was doing in that area. When I told her, she said "I'm a counselor on the sixth floor. You're not supposed to be here. However, if you didn't know, I'll excuse you this time." She wheeled away, obviously a stern disciplinarian. I went upstairs to wait until I saw other women proceeding to the elevator. My experience may have been the exception, for several women told me that the YWCA was a good place to stay because the rules were less rigid than at the mission, and each woman has her own room.

A third place that a woman may find emergency shelter, and the largest shelter for women in the Baltimore area, is the one run by the Salvation Army, a worldwide organization of men and women who consider themselves to be in the Army of Christ. One of the services that this organization provides is shelter for the homeless. Most urban dwellers are familiar with the kettles and uniformed attendants ringing bells in shopping malls and on street corners during the Christmas holidays. This is one of the ways that the Salvation Army raises money, but it is also a member of United Way and accepts donations of goods from business and industry.

This shelter, with 38 beds for women, children, and two-parent families, is housed in a former mansion. The neighborhood consists of brownstone houses converted into apartments, offices, restaurants, and hotels. Three meals a day and clothing are provided, as well as counseling. Attendance at the worship services that are offered is not a requirement. Mothers and children are housed together in large bedrooms; an effort is made to keep families on one floor and single women on another, but that is not always possible. Women are allowed to stay for 21 days, but this may be renewed every 7 days if the situation is critical and other housing cannot be arranged. Because the Salvation Army is one of the few shelters that accepts both women with children and two-parent families, it is almost always filled. During snowstorms and freezing temperatures, cots are placed in the lounge and even in the dining room. Many of the homeless women of Baltimore begin their odysseys at this shelter.

When a woman's time in an emergency shelter expires, and if she is still homeless, a staff member at an emergency shelter will contact a transitional shelter and arrange for an interview. The staff members at the Salvation Army and the YWCA attempt to place women in transitional shelters that will meet the womens' needs. For example, deinstitutionalized women may be sent to the Park Avenue Lodge, and former prison inmates to Marian House. The transitional shelters have taken women on an emergency basis, however, if there are no other beds available. Even My Sister's Place has set up cots and allowed women to sleep on the floor during blizzards or other severe weather. At other times shelters may be more selective, for they are often not staffed adequately to handle the emotionally ill woman who is hallucinating, or the alcoholic woman who is drunk. They may refuse such women admittance. At transitional shelters the needs of the other women must be considered.

On one occasion I had the opportunity to visit the Salvation Army shelter with the coordinator of residential services of a transitional shelter. After interviewing two homeless women, one of whom was obviously fantasizing, the coordinator spoke to the director of the Salvation Army shelter and told her that she could not take the woman who had spent the previous two years in Springfield (a state mental hospital) and the last four months on the streets, but would take the woman who had just been released from a detox unit. The director seemed upset that the transitional shelter could not accommodate the deinstitutionalized woman, but the coordinator explained that she could not give the woman the attention that she obviously needed. The director and the coordinator of the transitional shelter are both concerned with homeless women, but their services are different and they have different perceptions of the problems.

Once a woman leaves an emergency shelter and is admitted to a transitional shelter, she can be assured of a place to stay. At the Women's Housing Coalition for example, a woman can stay for as long as one year, if she obeys the rules. The Women's Housing Coalition (WHC), after its success in establishing the Corner House shelter at the YWCA, realized that there was a need for long-term shelter. In 1982, the WHC opened Upton House and shortly thereafter also opened Howell and Lombard Houses. The WHC views itself not as a treatment facility or program, but as a provider of housing for single, low-income women. Using government and private grants, fundraisers, private donations, and funds from United Way to support the three houses, the coalition also charges each woman $100 a month rent. If a woman is not receiving any public aid, the WHC will assist her in applying for any benefits for which she is eligible.

Upton House is a transitional shelter that houses nine women. Consisting of two adjoining row houses that have been remodeled to contain a communal living-dining room, Upton House is located close to downtown Baltimore in a black neighborhood of row houses and housing projects. Women are allowed to stay at Upton House as long as one year if the service director feels the woman will benefit from such a stay. The average stay is eight months. Women at Upton House must have an income, usually General Public Assistance (GPA) or Supplemental Security Income (SSI), and pay a rent of $100 a month. The women are also expected to buy and prepare their own food.

The three houses sponsored by the WHC serve women who are well enough to function independently and do not need the daily attention or care of medical or psychiatric personnel. After a two-week probation period, a woman may sign a contract and stay for six months. After that time, the contract can be renewed for another six months (See Appendix 5). Some women eventually get jobs and are allowed to stay at the shelter until they have the financial means to get their own places to live. Guests are encouraged to feel that this is their home. Some of the residents are in programs such as Alcoholics Anonymous, some visit their psychiatrists weekly, and others have jobs. No one is required to vacate the house during the day. The service director acts as a counselor for the women, as well as assists with securing work and finding an apartment. The goal of the WHC is to assist a woman "through her immediate crisis into a more stable situation."

The rules focus primarily on housekeeping responsibilities, interpersonal relations, and safety and security. Like Karis Hospice and the YWCA, there are certain rules that if broken, are grounds for immediate dismissal. Drunkenness, violent behavior, and having visitors in a bedroom are examples of such infractions. Lee, a resident at Upton House for a brief time, was a white woman in her mid-forties, originally from Delaware. She had spent the last four years in Baltimore. An alcoholic, she had moved from shelter to shelter with time in-between spent in detoxification units. She left the detox and went to a night shelter that later moved her to a transitional shelter until her next binge. Then she was picked up by the police and sent to a detox again. She had completed one year of college and had wanted to be a nurse. When she could, she worked as a nurse's aide. She was on SSI because of a disability that she did not identify. She described her day at Upton House as follows:

> *I get up in the morning and on two mornings of the week I go to Constant Care Medical Center from ten to twelve for AA meetings. Sometimes I stay here [in the shelter] and watch tv or do laundry and talk to the other women. Some days I visit friends who are in AA, too. I was referred to Upton House by the detox.*

Seven days later she went into delirium tremens (DT's), caused by alcohol poisoning. The public health nurse took her to a local emergency room. Because drinking alcohol is not allowed at Upton House, Lee did not return.

Alisha, another resident at Upton House, described how she spent her days:

> *I usually get up when I feel like it, sometime around eight or nine. I fix my breakfast and then I wash my dishes. Then I sit and talk to anybody else who's here or watch the television. I might do my laundry or go back to my room. I read my Bible every day. I write to my children in West Virginia. Sometimes Ann and I might go to the store to buy cigarettes—I buy those generic kind cause they're cheap, but I really don't like the taste. I spend a lot of the day talkin' to Ann, and sometimes we go to the market or to the West Side Shopping Center. In the evening after I cook my dinner and clean the dishes, I talk to the other women or watch more television. Now sometimes I have to go to DSS [Department of Social Services] for my welfare [to check with her social worker].*

When she got tired, she went off to her private room on the third floor of the house and would take a nap. The freedom at Upton House allowed her to spend her time as she chose.

Dot, another resident at Upton House for ten months, got a job as a cleaning woman and laundress at a downtown nursing home. Because she had a job, her life took on the structure of working people with a regular time to get up, shower, eat breakfast, and go to work. Her evenings, after she fixed her dinner and cleaned up, were spent styling her hair, laundering her own clothes, watching television, and studying for the General Equivalency Diploma (GED) exam she hoped to take one day. On weekends she was a night supervisor at Marian House and a volunteer at My Sister's Place. That same freedom at Upton House allowed Dot the independence to accomplish her goals and to rejoin the mainstream. In December 1986, Dot moved into her own apartment. She said, "It was the freedom at Upton House that helped me reach the point where I could be on my own." Several women found this lack of structure a way to test their own strengths. In other words, if they could continue on their way back into the mainstream without supervision, then they were really ready. One woman told me that Upton House was "like a home" and another said that it gave more than "basic needs—it gave fellowship." Almost all of the women liked the

The evening entertainment at the Women's Housing Coalition.

coordinator of residential services [she has since quit her job] and found her to be helpful because she took time to listen and cared about the women. The word *support* was mentioned numerous times in reference to the coordinator.

Some women need more structure than Upton House provides. Marian House, another transitional shelter, is a joint project of the Sisters of Mercy and School Sisters of Notre Dame. It is supported by voluntary contributions, Catholic Charities, United Way, and a portion of each resident's income if she has any. The intent stated in its brochure is to accept "women who want to help themselves." Housed in a former convent, the shelter is located two blocks from Memorial Stadium in a blue-collar neighborhood. Sixteen women are in residence in a homey and well-furnished building. The screening process consists of two interviews. If the staff believes that a homeless woman can benefit from the program at Marian House, she is invited to have dinner with the other residents. After her departure the residents decide if she will be admitted. Their acceptance of her is the final approval for her admittance to a 2-week probation period. If she successfully completes the probation period, she will contract to remain for the next four months. This time can be renewed for an additional, and final, four months.

The staff at Marian House consists of a director, a personnel counselor, and a secretary. There are also two night supervisors, one on duty each weeknight and one on weekends. This shelter offers a highly-structured program and attempts to teach skills that will lead to independence. The brochure also states that Marian House will "help homeless and unemployed women discover their uniqueness and value as persons." Although this shelter is sponsored by religious orders of the Catholic Church, the emphasis is not on religious instruction. But the staff does show love, care, and concern. The philosophy is that the structured environment of Marian House is what women need in order to become self-sufficient and to leave homelessness behind them permanently. To accomplish these goals, residents are required to work with staff counselors who will help a woman obtain her GED high school diploma if necessary, find an appropriate job-training program, and develop resumes and interviewing skills and locate job opportunities. The staff also arranges for attendance at other programs outside the shelter that the woman might need such as AA, NA, or psychiatric counseling.

From the time a woman first approaches the staff for admittance, there is a set of rules to which the woman must adhere (see Appendix 6). Because a number of the residences are former prison inmates or deinstitutionalized women, the staff's objective is to provide the women with a sense of security. The women at Marian House never criticized the rules without noting that the restrictions were always tempered with love and concern. They viewed the rules as necessary to make the shelter work and therefore ultimately for their benefit.

The shelter houses 16 women in one building. For this reason, it is important that a new admission be approved by the residents. Although this undoubt-edly excludes women who need shelter, the women feel that this is the best way to determine if a woman will fit in with the other residents. The staff conducts a preliminary screening, and women whose speech and behavior are obviously irrational are not invited to attend the Friday dinner.

Cookie, an 18-year-old chubby blonde who looked like a Kewpie doll, described her stay at Marian House. For the first week, she was required, as are all new residents, to be inside by 6:00 p.m. and had to remain in Marian House for the first weekend. After the first week, the curfew is 10:00 p.m. during the week and midnight on Friday and Saturday nights. Cookie described a typical day:

> *Cookie: I get up every morning and I'm dressed by 8:30 a.m. because that is the rule. After breakfast there are household chores to do in the building as well as personal chores such as laundry and keeping my own room clean. I might meet with the counselor and we might have a house meeting tonight. I eat here every night with the other girls cause that's the rule. After supper I watch tv or talk or we might play cards or do each other's hair.*
>
> *Q: What do you do at house meetings?*
>
> *Cookie: We talk about problems. With all these people there are problems.*
>
> *Q: Can you give me an example?*
>
> *Cookie: Well, sometimes you don't like the chore you got assigned, like washing and waxing the floors too often, so you can ask for somebody to switch with you.*

Although there are disagreements among the women at times, the atmo-sphere is more like that of a sorority house than of a shelter. Cookie had been encouraged to set goals for herself and to work toward them with the help of the staff and the other residents. As a cross-addicted alcohol and drug abuser, she had been attending AA meetings seven times a week for two and a half months. She told me that Marian House gave her hope because she could see the prog-ress she had made by following the rules and working toward her goals.

Because of the structure at Marian House, some women are uncomfortable and choose to leave. The residents who participated in this study, however, were very positive about the shelter and its director, Sister Marilyn, who told me that the emphasis of the staff was always on care and concern for the women. The residents supported this, for they told me:

- This place has the structure that we need.
- It provides support.
- There is concern and care here.
- They take people in and give them a second chance at life.

- You're somebody important here.
- There's a lot of love in this house.
- I don't see her [Sister Marilyn] physical features. I only feel the warmth that she radiates.

For the 1988-89 fiscal year, Marian House had a total of 51 women in its program. Of this number, 35 were discharged, of whom 25 were judged to be self-sufficient. Women whom I interviewed in 1986 were proud of the current residents who were taking courses and working at jobs. These role models gave hope to the other women. It seems obvious that Marian House is more than just a place to avoid the streets.

Although several of the transitional shelters will accept women who have been deinstitutionalized, many of the shelters will not accept women who have proven to be "troublemakers"—women who have become loud and verbally abusive or disruptive to other shelter residents. The Park Avenue Lodge was opened in November 1986 to serve the specific needs of "bag ladies," women who had lived in the streets for extended periods of time or who had run the gamut of shelters and were no longer welcome. Catholic Charities, which operates the shelter, leased nine rooms from the Methodist's Women's Lodge, a women's hotel. A director and assistant, as well as volunteers, administer to the needs of the guests. Nancy Clark, the director of the Lodge when it opened, believed that "through love and support, we are able to empower women to begin the struggle to redirect their lives." Although some of the women may exhibit bizarre behavior at times because of their illnesses, they are treated with kindness and patience and as individuals. The Lodge has a separate living room set aside for the shelter guests and laundry facilities are available. Breakfast and dinner are served on the premises. Women are allowed to keep their possessions in their rooms.

One of the factors that varies from shelter to shelter is the amount of privacy. This, too, affects a woman's behavior in obvious as well as subtle ways. At Karis Hospice, where ten women may be sleeping in one room, the only privacy is in the bathroom. Most adult women are not used to such communal living, and the tossing and murmuring of others throughout the night can make sleeping difficult. Also, the number of beds in a relatively small room does not allow a woman to have a chest or dresser on which to display any personal belongings. For this reason, and because a woman must take her possessions with her in the morning, she makes no effort to establish a space that is her own. No photographs are set out, no remembrances of a former life.

The YWCA, on the other hand, provides private rooms for the women. There is no effort, however, to make the rooms homey: the walls are barren of pictures, there are no curtains on the windows, and there are no bedspreads. If a woman stays longer than three days, she may place her personal belongings around her room, but without curtains and rugs the room still has the appearance of a cell.

It is only in transitional shelters, where women stay for months at a time and where volunteers contribute items such as bedspreads and curtains, that women feel at home and take pride in their surroundings. Women who participated in the Upton House art classes (which will be discussed later) had their drawings on their walls months later. They kept photographs of their children and other mementos on their dressers and nighttables. They attempted to personalize their rooms and to make them as attractive as possible. This was true of the women at Marian House also. Simply stated, the women were making their rooms into homes.

Although most homeless women stay in shelters, some women do spend time in the streets before or after they have stayed in shelters. Yvonne, a 26-year-old black woman who has been institutionalized several times, lived in the streets one year from April to December.

Q: Where did you stay at night?

Yvonne: It depended on the weather. If it was warm I stayed at the park [would not tell me which one]. If the weather was bad, I stayed at different places. I used to stay at the bus stations and wash up there, but then they changed and said you had to have a ticket or you can't sit down or use the bathroom. The Y wouldn't take me—twice they wouldn't let me stay. The Salvation Army—they put me out after one night. I slept in Charles Center. It's warm in the winter—there's heat in the sidewalk grates.

Q: Were you afraid living in the streets?

Yvonne: Yes. I was afraid I would be raped or killed. There are sick people living in the streets.

Q: Was there anything else you were afraid of?

Yvonne: The cold. When I was arrested for trespassing it was because I needed a place inside. I know that a lot of people die on the streets each year.

Dot, who eventually found MSP and was then sent to Marian House, used a variety of places as shelter. While she was on drugs, she spent four months either sleeping at a friend's house, staying with a guy, or as she told me:

Dot: I walked the streets all night because I didn't want to go to certain people's houses. I stayed on a corner, I'd sleep for a while in a restaurant. Here, there, and everywhere.

Q: Why didn't you go to a shelter?

Dot: I didn't know anything about shelters. I could have been helped earlier, but I didn't know.

One deinstitutionalized woman spent six weeks on the streets of New York before she got into a shelter. She described her experience to me:

I lived on the streets for about six weeks. It was by the grace of God that I wasn't killed. I was robbed of the $50 I had. Then I got into a shelter. The food was terrible. I've never seen such food. They treat those people like animals compared to here. There was no privacy and men were walking through. It was awful; I was so frightened.

Henrietta told me that she had slept in vacant houses, parks, and empty cars because "the missions gave me the run around." She is an alcoholic who had been homeless for at least three years. Whether or not these stories of living in the streets are accurate, they are readily believed by other homeless women, and one of their greatest fears is that they will have to sleep in the streets.

For the majority of women, shelters are preferred even if the women do sometimes complain about the facilities. A major difference between homeless men and women is that men will sleep in the street more readily than women because a woman considers it dangerous to sleep in the streets. Also, most women do not think it demeaning to stay at a shelter; unlike the tramp culture that places emphasis on male independence and views men who stay at missions as weak, women are primarily concerned with the safety that shelters offer. When one woman who had recently obtained an apartment sneered at another woman who was staying at a shelter, the woman at the shelter said, "Well, at least I'm not staying in the streets."

Another difference is that male tramps consider their counterparts who stay in missions to be the weakest of all tramps because they are dependent on handouts. In Baltimore, men have refused to spend time in the mission shelters because they are "dirty and dangerous" (Breakey & Fischer, 1985, p. 18). None of the women ever commented about danger or dirt in the women's shelters, nor did they criticize women who stayed in shelters or in the streets. The example cited above was made by a woman who had moved out of shelters into what she hoped was a permanent residence. On the contrary, women only expressed sympathy or pity for any woman who was in the streets or who found herself in a shelter.

A third difference is that the shelters for women in Baltimore are small while those for men, the Helping Up Mission and the Baltimore Rescue Mission, have shelter for 123 and 150 men respectively. Also, there are few transitional shelters available for men. Sister Pat of MSP provided the reason for small women's shelters when I asked why Baltimore City didn't convert some of its closed schools into shelters. She responded, "We don't want to warehouse people. There is no dignity. Catholic Charities wants smaller places where there can be warm human contact." The homeless women of Baltimore seem to concur.

In addition to shelters providing beds, there is also a daytime shelter for women called My Sister's Place. It opens at 9:00 a.m. and closes at 4:00 p.m. The mission provides no meals, although instant soup, coffee, and tea are always available. The shelter is located in the heart of the downtown business district and a block from the largest soup kitchen in the city, Our Daily Bread. My Sister's Place is sponsored by Catholic Charities and United Way. Sister Pat McLaughlin was in charge of the day shelter when it opened. She told me that the staff "treats each woman as a unique person. No one is hopeless, nor is there any problem without a solution." She also said, "We try to give a woman what she thinks she needs, not what *we* think she needs."

The first floor of My Sister's Place consists of a large living room and dining room with a sink and a refrigerator, but no stove. There is also an area where a woman can leave her bags if she wishes to leave the shelter for a few hours. There are two free phones available for the women. The second floor contains a room for the children to play in, the clothing room where the women receive three outfits every two weeks, a washer and dryer, and showers. The staff consists of one nun, five paid staff members, and female volunteers.

Approximately 200 to 250 women come to MSP every week. The shelter attempts to provide shelter from the weather as well as hospitality and information. If a woman has no shelter for the night, a staff member will call the various night facilities in the city and try to arrange for the woman to stay at one of them. It is My Sister's Place that so often acts as the channel for the homeless women in Baltimore to find shelter and a bed for the night.

FOOD

Second in importance to shelter for the homeless woman is food. Although the media has focused on the "bag ladies" who eat from garbage cans and dumpsters, this is not the source of food for most homeless women. Even Yvonne, who lived in the streets, used other food supplies. When I asked her where she got her meals she replied:

Yvonne: I'd get up and eat breakfast at the Franciscan Society. They weren't open enough days and there's so many people—you have to have more than one meal a day. Then I'd go to My Sister's Place. I'd eat lunch at Daily Bread. Sometimes I'd go to Harbor Place and sit. You hope that someone will leave part of a lunch.

Q. What would you do if someone did leave a lunch?

Yvonne: You wait until they leave and then wait to see if they are coming back.

My Sister's Place.

Then you take it before the cleaning people come. Sometimes I got caught and was put out.

Yvonne had learned of the soup kitchens and usually used them. Only one woman, Henrietta, told me that while she lived in the streets she had "eaten out of dumpsters behind restaurants" and that "even animals do that—so will people to survive." For female drug addicts who are living in the streets, such as Pam before she came to Marian House, malnutrition is a strong possibility. Pam, who is approximately 5′ 8″ tall, said, "I didn't eat at soup kitchens. I drank a soda or [sic] potato chips. I weighed ninety pounds when I came here."

Most of the soup kitchens are supported by funds and volunteers from various churches in the city although they are non-denominational in their services. One such facility began in a woman's kitchen and then moved to a local church when the crowds grew too large (McCord, 1986). Another soup kitchen in west Baltimore is a former nine-bed shelter for women and children that a former seminarian and a former nun, now husband and wife, ran for five and a half years before converting the building to a food pantry and soup kitchen (Young, 1986).

Some soup kitchens, such as Paul's Place, rely on donations of food by local food stores and bakeries for a major portion of their supplies, but the balance must be supplied by churches. Paul's Place, affiliated with the Episcopal church, serves approximately 175 people at each meal and 7000 people a month (Chisolm, 1987). Our Daily Bread, run by Associated Catholic Charities, is Baltimore's largest soup kitchen, serving a midday meal to 400-600 people each day. Volunteers prepare and serve a hot dinner.

An additional soup kitchen that takes the food to the homeless is the Salvation Army's Feedmore program, a mobile soup kitchen that began operating in the fall of 1986. Soup, coffee, and sandwiches are served by volunteers to as many as 150 people each evening Monday through Friday from 6:30 to 8:30 beginning the first of each November and continuing through the end of April. The canteen moves to three downtown locations and one location in east Baltimore. Blankets and clothing are also given to the people who come to the canteen, for this may be their only contact with a service agency.

At Christmas and Thanksgiving, special holiday dinners with turkey and all the trimmings are prepared and served at the major soup kitchens. At other meals at Our Daily Bread, ample portions are given out, but there is a heavy reliance on noodles and macaroni because they are inexpensive. Fresh fruits and vegetables seem to be a luxury and are served only on special occasions.

In addition to the soup kitchens, many emergency shelters such as the YWCA and the Salvation Army serve three meals a day. Thus, once a woman is admitted to either of these shelters, she is assured of eating on a regular basis. Karis Hospice serves dinner and breakfast. A typical dinner might consist of baked beans, mixed vegetables left from the day before, bread (no butter), coffee, iced tea (no ice), and packaged sweets such as fruit pie or cupcakes. Breakfast would consist of cereal, bread, and coffee. Once a woman leaves Karis in the morning, she must either eat lunch at a soup kitchen or do without because she will not reenter the shelter to eat another meal until 4 p.m. Many women who stay at the Mission go to Our Daily Bread because it is centrally located and well known among the homeless. Women from the Salvation Army shelter also eat there if they are spending the day at MSP because it is too far to walk back to the Salvation Army just for lunch. The one-block walk from MSP to Our Daily Bread makes it the logical provider for the midday meal, and its reputation for serving good food makes it a popular place to eat. Usually several of the women will go there at 11:00 a.m. when it opens, eat the meal, and then return to MSP and tell the other women what was served. Our Daily Bread serves men and women. After waiting in line for the soup kitchen to open, the men in line allow the women to enter first "so they don't have to stand in the streets," an interesting act in the light of women's liberation and the gradual disappearance of the "ladies first" behavior that has existed in the mainstream.

The women, combined with personal observation, provide a description of the midday meal at Our Daily Bread. A woman entering receives a ticket and is then seated at a table set aside for women and children. The room is rather quiet, except for the sound of cutlery and dishes being moved. A volunteer brings the woman a plate on which all of her food is served. I have heard no complaints about this soup kitchen from anyone who has eaten there. This is not simply because these people are so hungry that they do not complain. They have commented that the food is "tasty" and "there is plenty and they sometimes give you extra desserts." A typical meal might be a casserole with noodles, beef, chicken livers, peas and carrots, plus a biscuit with butter, a piece of cheese, a danish, a glass of warm tea (even in summer), or coffee. The food varies from day to day, for it is prepared by a group of volunteers from a different church each day. When the woman finishes, she takes her dishes and flatware to a station where there is a trash can and a place to put the dishes. A volunteer cleans the table and replaces the flatware and napkin for the next guest. Daily Bread serves this midday meal from 11:00 a.m. to 1:00 p.m. If a homeless woman cannot get to Our Daily Bread during this time period, she may not eat during the day. The majority of guests at Our Daily Bread are homeless, but some women continue to frequent the soup kitchen after they have a subsidized apartment or are living in a transitional shelter because this helps them stretch their welfare dollars. Although the meals are not necessarily nutritional and include an abundance of starches because they are cheap, they provide a substantial and filling noontime meal.

Some women in transitional shelters must use food stamps to buy their food and then prepare it. Single women on welfare receive $90 a month in food stamps. I had the opportunity to observe how a woman obtains the stamps and how she uses them. On a hot and muggy August day, I drove Ann and Alisha,

Looking out at the line from Our Daily Bread.

residents of Upton House, to the food stamp office, a round trip of 19 blocks. The food stamp office was at the end of a short hallway that opened off the street. Two side-by-side glass booths were occupied: each contained a man behind thick glass with a mouth hole and a drawer. Ann explained to Alisha that she should show her ID (a non-driver's license with a photo on it) and her voucher from DSS (a piece of paper that looked like a money order). This produced books of food stamps from the man in one of the glass booths. When I asked Ann what Alisha could get with the stamps, Ann said that she could buy "anything edible but no soap, paper products, or dog food." The man in the second booth sold Maryland lottery tickets, bought by neither Ann nor Alisha.

When we left the building, I asked where Ann shopped. She said that the women usually went to Our Market, located about seven blocks away from the food stamp office. There is a small grocery store a half a block from Upton House but the women do not shop there if they can avoid it. On another occasion I had asked what a woman had paid for the items in a bag she purchased there. The items are listed in Table 1.

For this reason the women tried to shop elsewhere for their food. I offered to take Ann and Alisha to Our Market, and they readily accepted the offer of a ride and the opportunity to buy groceries without having to carry them the nine and a half blocks back to Upton House.

While at the store, Alisha bought items by planning aloud her menus for the next week, and Ann occasionally suggested items that would be easy to cook or that were on sale. The items bought by each woman consisted mostly of easy to serve foods. For a total of $12.00, Ann bought the following: Oodles of Noodles (5), lettuce, bread, Spam, soup, lunch meat, coffee, and canned spaghetti. Alisha, who spent $17.73, bought: Oodles of Noodles (10), ground beef, Coca-Cola, frozen broccoli, large sardines, canned soup (7), lettuce, tomatoes, soap, and plastic bags. Alisha paid for the soap and plastic bags with money from a welfare check; Ann is receiving SSI. Alisha planned to use the ground beef to fix dinner for Ann, two of the other women who had "been friendly," and herself.

Several factors affect the women who use food stamps. For example, the high prices at a nearby store are an external force that causes a number of the

TABLE 1 Comparison of items bought in grocery stores

Items	A nearby store	Our market
1 gal milk	2.10	1.89
4 oz. coffee	3.95	3.00
1 small Preem	1.40	1.00
1 Vienna sausage	1.75	1.00
Total	$9.20	$6.89

women at Upton House to want to shop elsewhere, even though the distance to Our Market is often a great inconvenience. Additionally, a lack of knowledge of nutrition combined with a limited knowledge of cooking results in women buying convenience foods that are easily prepared. Even though many of these women have large amounts of time during the day in which to cook, they usually prepare foods that are fried or heated on the stove in a short period of time. The reason for this is that there are only two stoves at Upton House for nine women to use. There simply is not enough time in which to prepare elaborate meals. Only occasionally do the women prepare meals together or for each other, but on many occasions I saw them share what they had.

The women at Marian House prepare their own breakfasts and lunches, but dinner is a communal meal. The dinners are prepared by the residents on a rotating basis, and a woman has to do her share during the eight months she stays there. Some of the meals are better than others because the cooks are better, but there is always plenty, and usually it is very good with special treats like homemade cakes or pies. Compliments are abundant if the dessert is special. Because of the variety of cooks, the food is also varied in preparation and, therefore, taste. The women seem to take pride in their efforts and want to do well at this assignment. The food is served family style with several women bringing the bowls and platters to the table. The requirement that the women eat this one meal a day together forces them to interrelate with one another, unlike Upton House where eating can always be a solitary affair. It should be pointed out that because Marian House has 24-hour staff on the premises, and the night supervisor dines with the women each evening, this requirement can be enforced. Because the coordinator at Upton House leaves each evening around five, before the evening meal, such a regulation cannot be enforced.

For many homeless women food is not only sustenance for life but also a topic of conversation. During my time as a volunteer at the the Women's Housing Coalition and at My Sister's Place, I have heard women discussing food and recipes. Magazines at MSP such as *Good Housekeeping* and *Better Homes and Gardens* are perused, and dishes that sound tasty are described to others. As has been stated, the meals at Daily Bread are described in detail by those who eat first and return to My Sister's Place. When I baked several cakes for the women at Upton House, they asked me to describe the ingredients.

By contrast, the men who eat at Our Daily Bread and from the Salvation Army canteen are interested in sustenance only and view food in terms of quantity. Most of the men request second helpings from the canteen, often packing the sandwiches in their pockets or backpacks. One man who lived in the streets not only ate two bowls of soup each night, but also brought an empty coffee can and asked the volunteer to fill it with soup. Although men occasionally comment on the taste, they usually accept what is offered without comment. The food these men eat is most often prepared by others and not themselves. The missions and even a small shelter such as Christopher's Place, a

Dinner at Marian House.

two-to six-week transitional shelter for 24 men, do not allow the men to cook. Instead, staff members prepare the food. Homeless men primarily "eat to live," and their interest in food focuses on its availability. By contrast, women identify with food because of their lives as wives and mothers. Even if they do not have access to stoves or food to cook, the discussion of food and meals seem to fit in with their roles as women.

CLOTHING AND APPEARANCE

The stereotype of the "bag lady" depicts a woman wearing layers of clothing regardless of the time of the year. Don't all homeless women carry their clothing on their backs? Aren't all homeless women dressed in rags with their feet clad in run-down men's work shoes? In actuality the majority of women attempt to present a clean and attractive appearance. The clothing a woman has available often depends on the circumstances under which she became homeless. An abused woman such as Alisha left with only two changes of clothing because of the haste in which she fled her husband. Erlene had only the clothes she wore and the pair of shoes on her feet when she came into a shelter because "everything had gone for drugs." As Henrietta, who had spent the last few years living

in the streets, told me, "I've moved around so much, all my things are gone."
For these women and others like them, the emergency shelters, as well as My
Sister's Place, have clothing available that has been donated by individuals and
businesses. A woman is usually provided with three outfits every two weeks, as
well as shoes, a handbag, underwear, and sleepwear. At the end of the two
weeks she may select three other outfits when she returns the first three.

The majority of women, however, consider clothing to be one of the most
important factors to keep or take with them they become homeless. Of the
women in the interview group, 65% listed clothing as most important; 44% of
the women in the questionnaire group considered clothing most important and
an additional 29% listed it in the five most important things that they took with
them when they became homeless, along with personal mementos. Clothing is
considered important because it is protection against the weather, but it also
provides a woman with an identity, while making a social statement. One
woman told me that if she had on nice clothes and was clean, she could sit in a
hotel lobby during the day and would not be noticed and asked to leave. In other
words, she could pass for a patron. Another woman at My Sister's Place spent
quite some time trying to find a handbag that would "go with" her shoes.
Homeless women may dress in clothes that are not color coordinated or stylish,
but they do their best to look like other women. Even in winter, when warmth
should be the most important factor, a woman prefers a coat that fits and, if
possible, looks attractive. Only one woman whom I have seen in the last four
years of this research dressed in a bizarre manner that attracted attention, wearing red from her hat to her shoes, each and every day. She had psychiatric
problems and was a well-known figure in downtown Baltimore, primarily because of her dress. By dressing in a standard fashion and being clean, however,
a woman can sit at Harbor Place, the Lexington Mall, or the Lexington Market
and blend in with the crowd.

The women who live in transitional housing also have clothing available to
them because of donations. The women at Upton House and Marian House
dress in attractive and clean clothes. Larger women do not always have as
extensive a selection as average-sized women, but efforts are made to secure
clothing for them. Blue jeans are popular with many women because they wear
well and are commonplace. Practicality is another consideration. Because
women in transitional shelters are encouraged to seek employment, special
attention is given to outfits that women can wear to job interviews.

For women living in either emergency or transitional shelters, availability
of certain clothes can be problematic. For example, sometimes shoes don't fit
perfectly, and often a woman sacrifices beauty for comfort because she will
spend so much of her time walking. High-heeled shoes may be appealing, but
low-heeled shoes will not cause as much pain. Stockings without runs are also
difficult to obtain because most of the time women do not donate stockings
unless they have runs. Winter boots are usually not discarded unless they are

worn out. Selecting clothes from those donated to a shelter is not the same as shopping at a store, but the majority of women take some care with their appearances. Jewelry also has great appeal for the women even though it is not necessary for survival. A donation of costume jewelry delights the residents at a transitional shelter because it will help them to look like everybody else.

Keeping clothing clean is not a problem for most of the women because most shelters, including My Sister's Place, encourage the women to do their laundry by providing washers, dryers, and detergents. Woolen clothing, however, must be dry-cleaned, an expensive luxury not available to most of the women. The women can wear a coat for a winter, but dresses and skirts must be cleaned more frequently. Spot cleaning is a partial answer. The majority of homeless women I have observed are clean and dressed neatly. Several months ago I took photographs of the guests at My Sister's Place (with their permission) and gave them copies. I also showed the photos to a group of middle-class suburban women who unanimously agreed, "They look just like us."

In addition to attempting to dress as mainstream women do, most homeless women care about their appearance in other ways. The majority of women keep themselves clean, although some of the deinstitutionalized women may neglect personal hygiene and not bathe. All of the shelters require the women to keep themselves clean. My Sister's Place has shower facilities and encourages the street women, who often do not have access to showers, soap, or towels, to bathe. But there are exceptions. The woman with matted hair who lived in an abandoned building and was using the Salvation Army canteen as her source of food had obviously not bathed for months. She was encrusted with dirt from her huge tangle of hair to her feet. She was noncommunicative except to ask for food, and it was difficult to determine if she was mentally ill.

Homeless women are also attentive to their hair. To see women at transitional shelters with their hair in curlers or giving each other haircuts is not unusual. At the Park Avenue Lodge a woman shampooed her hair one evening and then rejoined the group in the living room to watch television. At Karis Hospice three women put their hair in rollers or pincurls and two others shampooed their hair before going to sleep. At Upton House, Lydia became the resident hairdresser, although she had no training in this field. She liked to style hair and had some skill, and several of the other women allowed her to cut and set their hair. I have seen women's handbags and shopping bags at MSP that contained hair rollers, and one woman carried a hair dryer with her that was broken. Makeup is also valued, but because of its expense, women who have been homeless for any length of time may no longer have access to it. Younger women especially consider it important, for many of the women I questioned and interviewed wore makeup.

Homeless men, because of their transience and the fact that many of them are willing to live in the streets, are often unbathed and dressed shoddily. Numerous men who come to the canteen have hands that look as if they have not been washed for days; often their clothes are stiff with dirt. The men often have beards because they have no razors or other shaving supplies. For these reasons, the men are easily labeled as "bums." Clothing can be obtained at various shelters, but, as previously stated, the men often refuse to go to the shelters. The most frequently requested items from the canteen are hats and gloves. Socks, underwear, and sweaters are also in demand. The men want clothing in order to survive; whether the clothing is fashionable seems irrelevant, although they will refuse a hat or scarf if they think it is a "woman's" color or style. Warmth and comfort are their primary concerns.

It is true that homeless women are not the best dressed women in Baltimore, although that was the case in New York when Bloomingdale's featured the baggy, disheveled "bag lady" look in its store windows a few years ago. Homeless women have not created a mode of dress that is unique to their situation. Their first consideration is comfort, but appearance is not overlooked. Because of their attempts to blend in, most Baltimoreans do not recognize the majority of homeless women in their midst.

TIME

For most homeless women who have found shelter, time can stretch interminably throughout the day, interrupted only by meals. If a woman is on the streets her time may be spent as Yvonne's was:

Yvonne: Sometimes a man at Daily Bread would take me to a movie.

Q: But that wasn't every day?

Yvonne: No. Sometimes I'd go to the Walters Art Gallery. It was free then (there is now a $2 admission.) I learned to like paintings. In the summer I went to Druid Park Pool and went swimming. That's how I took my baths.

For women in emergency shelters the day may include going to the Department of Social Services (DSS), located on Greenmount Avenue. Even for women staying at the Salvation Army shelter, which is closer than some of the other shelters, the walk to DSS is approximately 20 blocks round trip. Thus a trip that might take 15 minutes round trip in a cab takes 45 minutes to 1 hour on foot. If a woman wants her welfare check and her food stamps, she will take the time to visit DSS and her social worker, for it not only assists her in getting money and food stamps, but also fills the time. A woman staying at the Karis Hospice who wishes to spend the day at My Sister's Place, eats lunch at our Daily Bread and returns to the hospice has walked approximately three miles. If she wishes to stop at DSS, that will add another two miles to her journey. Because there are no direct bus routes involved nor money for public transportation, walking is the primary mode of mobility. In pleasant weather the women go to Harbor Place, Lexington Market, or Lexington Mall. Here they can blend in with the crowds, find a bench on which to sit and "people watch" because it passes the time. If the weather is bad, however, many of the women who are staying in emergency shelters will usually spend part of the day at MSP.

Although few women indicated that they had learned homeless patterns of

Woman on a bench.

behavior from other women exclusively, many women who frequent My Sister's Place share information. A conversation that I overheard provides an example. One woman was discussing why she couldn't get a "Section 8." Another woman asked what a Section 8 was. The first woman replied, "That's where the government pays most of your rent for you because the landlord agrees to let you stay there." The attention of the small group turned toward the new woman, and one woman asked if she was on welfare or SSI. These terms were also unfamiliar to the newcomer, and the other women explained them. One suggested that she go to "the welfare" and gave accurate directions. In this way women learn what services are available and where. This can explain Henrietta, who was staying at the Salvation Army shelter and had emphatically stated that no one had "taught" her anything about being homeless and that she had learned on her own, nevertheless had eaten at soup kitchens, had called missions "who gave [her] the run around," and had been sent to the Salvation Army by the South Baltimore General Hospital detoxification unit. The implication seemed to be that although no one had taken her in hand to explain where to eat and stay, she had overheard other women and had been able to survive for several years as a homeless woman.

Time at MSP is spent in a variety of ways. There was no television set there at the time of this study: one of the assistants explained that there would be disagreement about what to watch because there may be 75 or more women in the shelter at one time. Some women sit and stare out the window; others play cards; a few sit and talk to each other; one fixes a cup of coffee; another takes a shower; some wash clothes or exchange clothes for a new set; some may talk to one of the staff members who arrange for shelter, counsel the guests, or help them in other ways; several use the telephones (which are free) to apply for jobs, talk to relatives, or look for a place to stay; some women sit in the upholstered chairs and sleep. One woman who now has her own apartment in subsidized housing told me:

> I still come here. I still need the friendship I find here. I'm alone in my apartment. When I run short of clothing, I can go upstairs [to the clothing room]. I feel happy when I'm here.

If the weather is bad, the women might go to the central branch of the Pratt Library and spend time reading the newspaper or some of the magazines, but the library does not encourage this. However, if a woman is not offensive, that is, does not smell too badly, is not obviously drunk, or does not disturb anyone, she may stay at one of the large reading tables in a building that is warm in winter and air conditioned in summer. One woman told me, "I can't go to the Pratt. They put me out because I was drinking and made a fuss in there."

In addition to the central library, My Sister's Place is a touchstone for

women in emergency shelters who must often fill their days away from their
night shelter. Ada described one of her typical days while she stayed at Karis
Hospice:

> *I was called at 6:00 [a.m.], did a chore and then had breakfast and church. Then
> I walked to My Sister's Place and had coffee. I sat there for a while and then
> walked down to Lexington Mall [a pedestrian mall with benches two blocks from
> My Sister's Place]. It was nice so I sat on the benches for a while. Then I walked
> to Daily Bread. After dinner I went back to My Sister's Place. I used the newspa-
> per and the phone to try to find a job and a room. Then about 3:30 [p.m.] I start
> back to the Mission.*

She estimated that she walked three to five miles a day.

Women living in transitional shelters may have more time on their hands
than the women in emergency shelters. The women in transitional shelters
usually buy food for several days and have clothing, and they are not required
by the rules to leave their shelters during the day. The distance they walk per
day may not be as great as for those women who are staying in night shelters
and who must walk to all of the services they need. Most transitional shelters
also have televisions, and this helps women spend their time. Other than doing
laundry, cleaning the shelter, and cooking meals, the women in these shelters
spend more time in social activities. They may also spend time attending AA,
NA, or counseling sessions. For example, of the nine women at Marian House
whom I interviewed, eight were in these programs or seeing a psychiatrist.
Another way women spend time is attending to medical needs. When Alisha of
Upton House needed eyeglasses, Ann took her to the optician who had provided
Ann with glasses through Medicaid, an all-day trip by bus to a west Baltimore
shopping center.

The length of time a woman has been homeless may also determine how
she spends her time. Lily, who had been at Marian House only 17 days when I
interviewed her, described what she had done on most of those days:

> *I get up around 6:30 [a.m.] and listen to music. At 7:30 I have cereal and coffee
> and read the paper. Then I do my chores and clean my room. I see if anybody is
> around and talk to them. I go out for a walk. I have people to see here—you
> know, the counselor, like that.*

The boundaries of most of these women are very limited. For some of the
women at Upton House their world consists of a square composed of Pennsylvania Avenue to the north (Our Market). Greenmount Avenue to the east (Department of Social Services), Pratt Street to the south (the Inner Harbor) and
Mount Street to the west (Urban Services). This is a total of approximately one

and a half square miles. Because homeless women do not own cars or have money for bus fare, they usually walk. This is why they often shop where the prices may be higher, but the convenience is outstanding. It is also why they frequent the same soup kitchens, the same shopping malls, and the same areas of downtown Baltimore.

In order to leave homelessness behind, women must have the financial means to pay for rent and food. With the help of the staffs of the transitional shelters, several women at both Upton House and Marian House were either actively seeking work or had full-time jobs. Both of these activities filled large segments of time. For Carol at Upton House, who was about to move into her own apartment, time was filled with her job:

> *I get up at 6:00 [a.m.], go to work, work until 5:30 and come home [Upton House]. I fix dinner, watch tv. Some nights I do my laundry, clean my room. Then I go to sleep.*

Vanessa at Marian House spent most of her time while she was at the shelter in a program to renew her nurse's license. Four of the nine women at Upton House had jobs during the months I conducted interviews there. House meetings and organized social events also help fill the evening hours. In addition, trips to Oriole baseball games, biweekly art classes, cookouts in the summer, and time spent together in the evenings playing cards or board games help to pass the time.

The major reason that time hangs so heavily for homeless women is that without money options are limited. Once a woman visits her social worker and qualifies for her monthly checks, she has little to do to fill her time. Museums now charge entrance fees, and movies are expensive. The choices for women with no money for bus fare or lunch are severely limited. In addition, homelessness seems to sap the energy of these women. None that I saw exhibited a high-energy level, although many women I interviewed were young and seemingly healthy. Perhaps the trauma of their situation has drained them or left them depressed. Perhaps their diets are causing their lack of energy. Whatever the causes, time drags by for most homeless women.

Harry Murray's observations (1986) about the cyclical nature of time for homeless men are applicable in some respects to the homeless women in Baltimore. Three women whom I met at MSP received checks that allowed each to rent a cheap room at the beginning of the month. Between the fifteenth and the end of each month, they would be seeking space in shelters because their welfare checks would have run out. Except for the women who had jobs and weekly or biweekly paychecks, the other women marked time by the arrival of their welfare or SSI checks. One evening at Upton House, Vivian and Lydia commented with excitement about the arrival of their checks. Time is also marked by the hours of the soup kitchen, which play a major part in the lives of the women who eat there. Not only does this midday hour break the monotony, but it also can determine whether a woman eats two meals a day or three. Clearly, these women view time in a different way from people in the mainstream.

THE BAGGAGE OF HOMELESSNESS

The shopping bags are the accessories of today's homeless women that have provided a label for them—"bag ladies." Some people believe that women carry fortunes in their shopping bags, and this has caused a number of women whom I interviewed to be beaten and robbed. What most homeless women are carrying in their bags are their entire worlds. When a woman is displaced, it is necessary to select from among her possessions what is most important. If the person is limited to one or two suitcases or shopping bags, the selection reduces the items to those considered critical for survival, and also, as Spradley (1970) has pointed out, for personal and social identity. Spradley (1970) stated that for tramps, "Rings, watches, money, wallets, identification papers, address books, and clothing help to give structure to *who* one is . . ." (emphasis in original, p. 144). As Spradley has also stated, those tramps with the fewest possessions are the ones who are most respected, for this shows that they can live by their wits. The possessions of a homeless person can provide insight into similarities and differences between men's and women's possessions as well as into what the person values.

Local newspaper accounts about homeless men provided information about what they carried with them. One man carried everything in the four pockets of his Army jacket. This included a Zippo lighter, a pipe, a razor, toothbrush and toothpaste, a knife, fork and spoon, a tobacco pouch, lighter fluid, and a pair of pliers to open outside faucets (Ollove, 1986). Another man reported that his only possessions were a few dollars, a driver's license, a pair of pants, and several pairs of socks (Greene, 1986). Some men own only the clothes on their backs, even though there may be several layers. The men I have seen in Baltimore eating from the Salvation Army canteen have usually worn a backpack or carried two or three shopping bags. They also may have a blanket, especially when the weather is cold. The most requested items are underwear, socks, coats, blankets, and hats and gloves, depending on the weather. Occasionally, one can see a man with a shopping cart piled so high with plastic bags as to almost tip over, and with large plastic cans hanging from the sides, but these men are few and far between. For the most part, homeless men travel light.

When women become homeless, they attempt to take their belongings in suitcases, but this is not always possible because there may be none available. Plastic shopping bags are used because they are strong, durable, waterproof, and usually easy to obtain. The bags are crammed to the top and are very heavy because they may contain all of a woman's possessions. The plastic handles cut into the palms of the hands, and the weight causes muscles to ache, but the shopping bags are preferred to green garbage bags because they are easier to handle and to carry, and they are not as conspicuous. The shopping bags are used until they tear, and then every effort is made to replace them.

The backpacks the homeless men use to carry their possessions are designed for students and campers, and are out of place in an urban setting. A man carrying numerous plastic or shopping bags is also unusual enough in our society to cause passersby to take note. The bindle roll of the tramp has been replaced by the backpack and the shopping bag, but they are still distinctive signs of a wanderer. By contrast, the majority of homeless women, except for the severely disturbed woman in the streets, try to blend in with the mainstream by using an item that is as commonly used by women in public as the handbag— a shopping bag. Some few homeless women, however, also travel with nothing more than the clothes on their backs. This is usually because of circumstances and not by choice, as demonstrated by Erlene and Henrietta. Most women, however, take a number of things with them regardless of their reason for becoming homeless. The questionnaire that was given to 100 women as well as to the 22 women who were interviewed indicated the wide range of possessions that the women considered "most important for you to keep or take with you." The questionnaire allowed five spaces for responses and did not rank the items by number. The results are listed in Table 2.

One of the women interviewed said that the most important thing she took with her were her memories of her husband and three children. The women who answered only the questionnaire also listed other unusual "things" that they took with them such as: mementos; myself, alive; God; my son; and my children. These, too, like the women's memories, are intangibles that represent their lives before they became homeless. Whatever they have taken with them when they were displaced, they are keenly aware that these few bags of belongings are poor substitutes for what they may have had. One woman even responded, "At this point even the most precious items aren't important."

Although clothes have a high priority for women as they do for men, women also carry many items with them that are not necessary to survival in the streets. Makeup, nail polish, a stuffed toy duck, and a pillow are not the weapons one uses against the cold and starvation. Yet when I asked the women why they had made these choices, they all had explanations. The nail polish, makeup, or perfume "make me feel like a woman." One woman keeps a Christmas card that her 12-year-old son, the oldest of three, picked out and paid for with his lunch money: it says, "God bless you, Mother." Her three children are in the custody of their father because she has been institutionalized so many times during the last few years. Another woman has kept a stuffed toy duck for 24 years because her grandparents gave it to her when she graduated from high school. She lived with them for several years when she was abused by her own

TABLE 2 Possessions most often listed by homeless as "most important for you to keep or take with you"

Items listed	Interviewees $N = 22$	Questionnaire $N = 100$
Clothes	13	74
Shoes		3
Coat		2
Dresses		
Undergarments		
Toiletries		2
Makeup		
Toothbrush		5
Grooming aids		
Comb		2
Cosmetics		
Nail polish		
Perfume		
Documents	4	4
Marriage certificate		
Credentials		
Resumes		
I.D.	2	8
Portfolio		
Telephone numbers		
Social Security card		3
Driver's license		
Birth certificate		2
Important papers		5
Address book		
Personal items		3
Bible		8
Pictures	3	
Father		
Children		
Son		
Sister		
Grandmother		
Baby		
Husband		
Other	3	
Album		2
Plants		
Purse		
Radio		
Jewelry		
Pillow		
Suitcase		

TABLE 2   Possessions most often listed by homeless as "most important for you to keep or take with you" (*Continued*)

Items listed	Interviewees N = 22	Questionnaire N = 100
Personal items		
Cards		
.357 magnum		
Glasses		
Duck		
Books		2
Baby clothes		2
Medication		3
Wallet		
Pocketbook		
Children's toys		
TV		
Bedding		
Furniture		
Money		4
Watch		
Hygiene items		4

Note. Numbers not provided for each item. Each item appearing here was listed at least once. Respondents could list more than one item.

parents. Eileen has a little plaque that has lettered on it "Momma's Kitchen." It is packed away in a box until she finds her own place. The pillow is kept by 18-year-old Cookie, whose mother died when Cookie was 13. She told me:

> When my mother died, she had a feather pillow. When she died, I packed up the house, and I hid that pillow so that no one would put it with her other things that were going to be given away. I still have that pillow and pillowcase. I sleep with it. I suck my thumb. They [pillow and pillowcase] make me feel secure.

The majority of homeless women who have enough time when they are displaced to take shopping bags or suitcases with them do not pack with the idea of living in the streets, as do numerous homeless men. The belongings of the women indicate that they take items that have personal meaning to them, that often represent the life they are living when they must leave. Some of these are personal articles, while others may serve no practical purpose. One young woman carried several record albums with her, even though she did not have access to a record player. Another woman kept computer diskettes. The choices of the women represent fragile threads to a time when they had a "home." Perhaps all of the things that women take with them when they leave home help to make them feel secure.

Another distinction between male and female homelessness is that, unlike men who keep as few possessions as possible because they travel and possessions would be burdensome, the women in this study tried to take as much as possible with them when they were displaced. Clothes were especially important to the women, but they often carried as many bags as possible filled with numerous items. My Sister's Place provides lockers for women who have no other storage space. When Sister Pat showed me this area of the basement, she also showed me the overflow of plastic bags and battered suitcases crammed full with the possessions. Without further research into what the woman take with them and why, it may be premature to use the word "nest," yet this stereotypical behavior of females appears to have some basis in truth when applied to many of these women. It would appear that if these women cannot remain in the mainstream, many of them will try to take their "homes" with them.

OTHER AGENCIES

There are agencies with which homeless women come into contact other than shelters and soup kitchens. One of these agencies is the Baltimore City Police Department (B.C.P.D.). Dennis Hill (personal communication, February 20, 1987), Director of Public Information for the Baltimore City Police Department, stated that the police are not given any training for dealing with the homeless; however, during bad weather the officers are reminded of the homeless during the 20-minute roll call they receive before they go on duty. The policy of the department is to offer help such as calling an ambulance if the person needs medical help or bringing the person into headquarters in bad weather if the person is not lucid. If a homeless person is a "problem," for example, a drunk panhandling shoppers, the officer moves the person out of the area although "If we don't see them, we leave them alone," stated Hill. When asked if Baltimore's vagrancy laws dealing with loitering in public places are still enforced, Hill said yes. He then qualified his answer by explaining that the jails are overcrowded with serious offenders and "we don't have room for them [the homeless]. Ten to 15 years ago we would have locked them up; now we are more sensitive to the needs of the homeless."

During snowstorms and bitter cold the police stations are opened to the homeless who seek shelter. The police will give someone a cell if any are available. Otherwise, the police will allow the person to sit in the station house. The police call these people "lodgers" and in very bad weather there may be as many as a dozen "lodgers" in the entire city. In addition, the policeman on his beat will refer any homeless person he finds to a shelter or to the Department of Social Services. The policeman will also take an alcoholic to a treatment center.

New York, Boston, and Philadelphia have emergency policies requiring police and city employees to round up and take the homeless to shelters after the temperature drops below freezing (Alter & Stille, 1984). Hill stated that because of the possible infringement of the individual's rights, the Baltimore City Police Department, after a meeting with the American Civil Liberties Union, made a decision not to allow such a policy in Baltimore.

The police were not usually a topic that homeless women brought up, but one of the comments I did hear was, "They don't have too much concern for people in the street." I asked Yvonne, who had lived in the streets, how the police treated her.

At Harbor Place they treat you nasty. One night I slept in a phone booth and the police drove me out and sent me walking. When I was arrested for trespassing, they had me in jail for a week and then they sent me to Springfield [state mental hospital].

It should be pointed out that the majority of homeless women do not have contact with the police. For those who do, the experience may be negative because of the circumstances under which the two meet. That is, a woman may be arrested for such offenses as being drunk and disorderly, creating a disturbance, trespassing, or child abuse. Of the 22 women I interviewed, four women had been arrested for misdemeanors, one for each of the offenses mentioned above. In addition, another woman was arrested for assault with intent to murder, and still another served time for fraud. The majority of women seem to feel that the police do their job, and they have no resentment toward them. It could also be possible that the women feel that because of their situation, as either lawbreakers or as homeless women, they are in no position to complain. People with low self-esteem can accept negative treatment without complaint.

Another agency that is tied closely to the lives of homeless women in Baltimore is the Department of Social Services (DSS) or "welfare" as the women call it. Within the DSS the Emergency Environmental Service Unit is responsible for intake functions for "new" homeless people. According to Jeff Singer (personal communication, August 14, 1987), a former supervisor with DSS, the Income Maintenance Service administers AFDC (Aid to Families with Dependent Children) and GPA (General Public Assistant), food stamps, medical assistance, and emergency assistance grants. The Intake Service Unit provides crisis-oriented social services such as emergency shelter, medical care, psychiatric attention, food, clothing, and counseling. For example, a woman might call DSS when she becomes homeless. The Intake Service Unit finds emergency shelter, food, and clothing for her and then refers her to the Income Maintenance Unit. DSS often refers women to the Salvation Army shelter, Karis Hospice, Antioch House, the YWCA, and Project Plase. Singer estimates that DSS serves 3,000–4,000 people a year who are homeless; that there are 200–400 people in Baltimore who are sleeping outdoors; and that there are approximately 8,000–12,000 people a year who are served at shelters in Baltimore City.

The DSS is the distributor of many of the sources of income for which homeless women may be eligible. Each of these sources is designed for a different type of recipient. GPA, for example, is available to destitute, single individuals who are disabled, unable to work, and not eligible for AFDC, SSI, or other federal assistance. The amount in 1990 was $195 a month or $6.50 per day (Welfare Advocates, personal communication, August 1990). AFDC is for families in which children are deprived of support through a parent's death, inability to work, or absence; most AFDC families are headed by a single female. A mother and two children would receive $396 a month. SSI(Supplemental Security Income) is a federally-funded program for the aged, blind, and disabled. A totally disabled person in Maryland would receive $386 a month (Welfare Advocates, personal communication, August 1990). States are allowed to supplement SSI, but Maryland does not. An additional program, Food Stamps, is available to any of the categories listed above who fall under the federal government's poverty level. The GPA and SSI recipient would each receive $90 a month in food stamps.

As their major source of income through GPA, AFDC, or SSI the women have frequent contact with the agency. Those who are not homeless might expect that people who are desperate should be grateful and nonjudgmental of the help they receive. In November 1986, the Consumers Union Institute for Consumer Policy Research sponsored a conference on "Ending Poverty" at which Stephen Glaude (1986), Executive Director of the National Association of Neighborhoods, stated that "personal pride is the factor that gets people off of welfare and we should use the poor to design the programs" that affect them. Certainly the treatment that the women receive at DSS can affect that pride of which Glaude spoke. The majority of the comments from the women were negative. The women admitted their need for welfare, but many commented that there just wasn't enough money from Welfare to survive independently. One woman commented, "They don't hassle you but they don't help." Another said, "They treat us like we're homeless. They've got a home and a paycheck, and they act as if our money is coming out of their pockets." Two women told me that the social workers were nasty. Whether this is true or not, Welfare Advocates, an organization composed of the heads of agencies dealing with the poor and the homeless, pressured DSS to begin a five-hour training program for social workers in "communicating with the public with courtesy" in 1987. A group of five women at the Salvation Army shelter discussed "workfare," as they understood the federal government's program, one evening in 1987. Their consensus was that although they were able and willing to work, they needed to be paid a living wage "if they want us to get off welfare." Another frequent complaint was that it took too long to get welfare, and weeks might go by before a woman received any money. If the federal government is sincere about welfare reform, it would be worthwhile to involve homeless women in the making of policy. Homeless women could be paid as advisers on homeless issues to the Department of Health and Human Services as well as the Department of Housing and Urban Development.

Another agency that has some contact with the homeless is the Urban Services Agency. A merger of the Model Cities Agency and the Community Action Agency resulted in 1976 in the Urban Services Agency, which has 13 neighborhood centers. Its basic function is to administer social services and to meet needs not met by other agencies, such as loss due to fire, stolen clothes, lost food stamps, or other crises that might occur. Urban Services also works with the Department of Social Services Eviction Prevention Unit to help someone relocate who can no longer afford the rent on a particular home or to arrange for a small grant that might help prevent an eviction (Breakey & Fischer, 1985). The agency also can provide three days of food, and clothing. The agency usually does not see a homeless woman more than once because this is considered a one-time emergency.

In addition to agencies that provide food and shelter, there is a clinic in Baltimore that services the health needs of the homeless. In 1985, Health Care for the Homeless began offering the services of a professional medical staff and now occupies a building in downtown Baltimore where the homeless can get walk-in attention. A medical person also rides the Feedmore canteen of the Salvation Army one night a week to minister to those who may not know where the clinic is located.

The principal function that all of these agencies offer to the homeless is support, usually in the form of material things. The homeless know that there is more that is needed than simply other people giving them things, no matter how well-intentioned the givers may be. However, the homeless are seldom included in the planning and designing of program to serve their needs, nor do they sit on the boards of directors of service providers. They do have very definite ideas about what they need if they are to overcome homelessness on a permanent basis. The word *support* and the need for support were mentioned over and over again by the women in this study. The type of support they were talking about was a network of caring and nonjudgmental people. These women know the lives they have led, the personal problems that have caused them such pain and deprivation of home, family, and friends. They want assistance, not recriminations. If assistance is offered early enough, it might help break the cycle of homelessness in which some women find themselves. Whether that assistance comes in the form of paid staff counselors or regular house meetings of residents, the women can be secure that they are not facing their problems alone, and that there are human resources available to them. The women at Marian House are grateful to a staff that helps them set personal and vocational goals. The women at Upton House are treated as adults and are encouraged to think of the house as their home. Ann told me, "I never felt homeless after I came here."

Marian House, the Women's Housing Coalition, and the Park Avenue Lodge offer support through multiple staffing and long-range shelter. As one woman said, "You cannot get yourself together in three days or even three weeks." This was echoed by several women. As demonstrated by the records of these two transitional shelters, when women are given time to recuperate and given support to help them step-by-step, they can rejoin the mainstream and have an excellent chance for remaining there.

HOMELESS WOMEN AND THE MAINSTREAM

Numerous studies (Allsop, 1967; Flynt, 1972; Harper, 1982) have shown that many men have enjoyed the freedom and lack of responsibility that homelessness can produce in them. The lure of the open road, the need to survive only for the day, and the opportunity to ignore rules have appealed to some men. This has been documented by the above-mentioned studies. This is not the case with homeless women. Not one woman I interviewed and not one questionnaire reflected anything but despair and distaste for the situation in which the woman found herself. No woman wanted to be homeless. Even the women who had left their homes voluntarily, such as abused women, wanted again to have a home, but under different circumstances. The most independent and strongest women to whom I spoke wanted their own places in which to live. Over and over I heard, "Well, I never had to be in the streets, thank God." Regardless of the age of the women, they did not think of this as some great adventure. They were acutely aware that life in the streets is very dangerous, and that in a shelter they were safe for the night at least. They all expressed regret and even shame for their homelessness and the personal failure they feel that it represents. One woman said to me, "If this is as far down as I can go, I'm glad this is it."

Because of their distaste for their lives as homeless women, they cling to the fringes of the mainstream. They desperately want to rejoin their former worlds in which middle-class roles and values have been assimilated by those of the lower class. By dressing like mainstream women and carrying shopping bags rather than other containers, they do not stand out in a crowd. By bathing, taking care of their appearance, and keeping their clothing presentable, they can convince the rest of the world and, equally important, themselves, that they can be the same as other American women.

It is for this reason that they attempt to create a semblance of a home with the mementos that they have brought with them. Even if they are single women, they had a place that was theirs at one time. The personal items that the women bring with them are links to their pasts. Anyone who wishes to begin a new life and disappear from the old one can do so without difficulty. These women, by contrast, take documents with them to substantiate not only who they are but also who they were, another link to the past.

The women in the transitional shelters have the opportunity to cook, and this reinforces their roles as the preparers of food, a role to which most of these women are accustomed. In a group discussion held one evening at the Salvation Army with five guests, one of the women said that she had volunteered to help with the cooking when she first came to the shelter, but was told that she couldn't. Another woman said:

Women with kids have to go to Welfare and even go to find jobs sometimes. We don't want to take them [the children] with us, but there's no choice. If we had a day care here that the mothers ran, I could leave my baby here today, and then tomorrow I could be in charge and another mother could go.

The women want to keep their roles as wives and mothers.

Their desire to maintain a facade of mainstream life is also exemplified by the ways in which they spend their time. Once they have arranged for Welfare and food stamps, they either spend time in finding more permanent shelter or they socialize with other women. Women in transitional shelters spend their time grocery shopping, watching television, cooking, and cleaning. They almost appear to be ordinary housewives, waiting for their husbands to arrive home from work. The difference is that there are numerous other women in the shelter doing the same things, and there will be no husbands arriving for the evening meal.

Although most women who spend daytime hours at the Lexington Mall, Lexington Market, and Harbor Place admittedly do so because they blend in with the crowd, and they can people watch, possibly another unvoiced reason is that these places are frequented by mainstream women. Thus a homeless woman can believe for a short period of time that she is just like the women who do have homes and families. Her daily patterns of behavior may say one thing. Yet as one woman said, "You have to have dreams." Her dreams may say something else.

6

SELF-IMAGES AND DREAMS

HOMELESS WOMEN VIEW THEMSELVES AND OTHER HOMELESS WOMEN

In the midst of a transient life in which there is no certainty, including the basic necessities, homeless women have not only fears but also hopes and dreams. Some of these are direct outcomes of their experiences as homeless women; others emerge from their culturally defined roles as females in mainstream America. Whatever their source, these shadows and fantasies are very revealing about the women, their lives, and their patterns of behavior. There are differences, for example, between the hopes of homeless men and those of homeless women. In addition, the dreams of the women do much to dispel the stereotypical belief that the women want to be homeless. Most revealing of all, perhaps, are how the women view themselves and each other.

One day at Upton House Alisha and Ann discussed marriage.

Alisha: I was discouraged from having a life of my own.

Ann: My mother said that to me, too.

Alisha: I was raised to believe that a woman should be a wife and mother.

Ann: I thought that woman's lib was awful. I don't feel that way now. [What changed your mind?] Who are you? Who am I? I mouthed what others said, and then I started to ask questions about myself.

Alisha: I think a man should respect a woman because she is a woman.

Ann: No woman should run her husband. A woman needs someone to fall back on. The man should be the buffer, the one to fall back on. [long pause] There's no respect for anybody or anything.

This dialogue seems to typify the backgrounds and beliefs of many homeless women. Although they may have heard of women's lib, its message of independence and self-actualization has had little impact on their lives. They continue to cling to roles and values that many women have abandoned, for, although many middle-class women are focusing on careers, homeless women still see themselves as wives and mothers, and the man as the breadwinner. There are exceptions, of course. Myla of Marian House and Carol of Upton House were raised in homes in which each was encouraged to develop her potential: Myla graduated from college and taught school, and Carol studied business in college for two years before quitting.

The majority of women viewed a woman's place as in the home, even though they no longer had homes. With the exception of two lesbians, 20 of the 22 women interviewed indicated past relationships with men. Half of this group was single, but even they felt "guilty" about not making it in the mainstream. Having "failed" in their roles as girlfriends or wives, which their backgrounds taught them to believe was the only meaningful role available except for that of mother, it is not surprising that they believe themselves to be "failures." Even women who had left their husbands because of abuse were negative about themselves. One woman said, "Most times it's your own fault. You can't blame other people."

Half of the women in this study had tried to live in the mainstream as married women. Stephen Crystal (1984) found that 71.3% of the men in his study were single. It should be noted that Crystal's study involved a male population of 5,609 men compared to the 122 women in this study. Nevertheless, a significant portion of the homeless women of Baltimore in this study have attempted permanent relationships within the mores of mainstream society.

Whatever their marital background, the majority of women indicated low self-esteem. Gilligan (1982) has observed that women see themselves in relationship to their connection with others. This can explain why many homeless women, some of whom have left even their connections with their children behind, are filled with such negative feelings about themselves. They revealed these feelings in isolated sentences that were scattered throughout their answers to other questions or as a response to a direct question such as, "How do you feel about yourself and your situation at this time?" Other comments were a part of their conversation as they discussed other things or told me about their lives. Some few viewed themselves as "better" than other homeless women:

I don't have much in common with these women—they aren't educated. I never had a support system. This is my last chance. The police have taken my child away from me twice.

I'm not the homeless type.

The majority, however, were quick to condemn themselves, ranging from one woman's ironic comment about her own birth to another's despair, so deep that only suicide seemed an answer.

I was born backwards (I was a breach baby) and I've been backwards ever since.

I'm self sufficient but I also tend to be self-destructive.

You can't live in the past. This is where I am. Where do I go from here?

I met guys, but none of them would take care of me. [What does "take care of" mean?] Feed [sic] and clothes. I wasn't one of the lucky ones.

I tried to kill myself. I didn't want to wake up. I feel good about myself now because it took a lot to walk out [on an abusive husband].

I was raised to be independent. I felt like I let everybody down when I left my husband. I failed.

There's anger, fear, and distrust in me.

I allowed others to manipulate me. I was raised not to show affection—to be brave. F____ that!

[Speaking about herself] This is a woman who has really screwed up her life.

I was a puppet on a string doing everything he told me to.

I hated myself. I still can't get over the fact that I'm twenty-six and living in a shelter.

I grew up without any sense of self worth.

I was a bum. I really was.

These negative self-images have resulted in suicide attempts for two of the women. It is not only finding themselves homeless that leaves the women depressed. Many of the women have also experienced sexual relationships that have ended in pain and trauma. One of the causes of homelessness for women is abandonment by a husband or boyfriend. Several of the women told me that it was the departure of a male and his financial support that resulted in their homelessness. The pain and trauma of separation from a partner, combined with finding oneself homeless, can be overwhelming.

In addition to living without their boyfriends or husbands, many of the women have also had to give up their children because the transitional shelters where they were staying did not allow them to keep their children with them. When a woman and her child leave an emergency shelter, she must either ask DSS to help her find housing, or she may be faced with the choice of temporarily giving up the custody of her child because there is a scarcity of shelters that take women and children. Approximately half of the interview group were mothers, although none of them had custody of their children. One of the women had grown children who were independent, and a number of the mothers had children who were living with their father or other relatives. One woman had her child in foster care, another had given her child up for adoption, and another did not know where her children were. They had done what they thought was best for the child at the time, as when Fay left her little girl with the father, a self-confessed flasher who was under court-ordered psychiatric care. Fay said, "He's good to her at least, and I can't even feed her." Lily told me that she left her baby with his father because "I was so messed up I was afraid I would hurt my son myself" even though her husband had abused Lily and once held a knife to the baby's throat. As one shelter provider stated, "Many of these women are having trouble keeping themselves together. How can they be expected to care for children?"

Yet by giving up their children, the women are separating themselves from an important part of their identities and reinforcing their images of themselves as failures, this time as mothers. If they cannot take care of their children, however, then someone else must, for three fourths of the children of these women were of dependent age. Wherever their children may be, the separation not only affects the way the women see themselves, but it also can provide their motivation to rejoin the mainstream, which will be discussed later in this book.

In addition to their recent troubled backgrounds, the majority of the women had lived in broken or troubled homes when they themselves were children. When I asked them to describe their childhoods, over and over they described families that were in constant turmoil, either from alcoholism or drug abuse on the part of one or both parents, separation of the parents, or other stressful events such a sexual and physical abuse of the child. For example, Vanessa was sexually abused by her father from the time she was a small child. Fay was the victim of her father's incest from the age of 3 until she was 14. She also had an alcoholic mother.

Less than half of the women had lived with both of their parents. Some had spent most of their childhoods with their single-parent mothers, while a small number had lived with either grandparents or another relative. Of those women who had been raised within the traditional family structure, two thirds reported that their parents' marriage had been "troubled." Bogue's research (1963), by contrast, found that 70% of the men in his study had come from what they described as happy homes. It is interesting to note that in spite of their troubled and unhappy childhoods, the majority of women had attempted to establish families of their own, compared to the large number of single men in Bogue's study. The unsettled backgrounds of the women, however, have contributed to the negative feelings they have about themselves because they often became the pawns in the struggles of their parents.

Although some of the women have spent time in jail, and others have been addicts, alcoholics, or institutionalized, it is their homelessness of which they are most ashamed. Again, their lack of connection to a home, may be the basis for this attitude. Even their terminology in talking about homelessness reflects their efforts to deal with their situation objectively. The term "bag lady" was never used by the women to refer to themselves, and I only heard one woman use the term when referring to other women. Instead, the women call them-selves "homeless" or "transient," or when speaking of those who live totally in the streets, "street people." A possible explanation of this is that those people working with the homeless in Baltimore do not use the term "bag lady" either. Some of the women seemed stunned by the fact that they were living in an emergency shelter; one of the women in a transitional shelter seemed to have difficulty accepting her surroundings, even though she had been in the shelter for several months. One woman, however, who had lived only in a transitional shelter, said that she was glad that she had never had to live in the other shelters because she had heard that "they were terrible."

Although the women expressed their views of themselves privately to me, I also wanted to know how they felt about each other. Many of them were very sympathetic. One woman told me:

Women have definitely gotten the short end. The women go back—to abuse, to drinking. A woman at My Sister's Place—her boyfriend threatened to kill her—she was thirty-five with three kids in Social Services [foster care]. She went back. Why can't women get up and go?

Another woman said, "Before I became homeless, I never knew there were so many women who lived like this." Others made the following statements:

It's not important how people become homeless.

Don't down people who are homeless.

No one wakes up one morning and says, "I'm going to be a transient."

They [homeless women] are scared and isolated.

A woman is not supposed to be on the streets. But it happens.

Women have just got to start dependin' on themselves. It's all right to be cared for and loved, but those men are just not out there right now.

Yet there were homeless women who were critical of the few women who live in the streets and do not seek shelter. One woman told me, "Most of them are there because they want to be, but not all of them." Another said, "There are women at MSP who won't take shelter. [Why do you think that is so?] I can't imagine why they wouldn't want shelter." Another woman informed me that some women will ask for money for "booze" and cigarettes, but the majority of women either disapproved of panhandling and would not do it, or were too embarrassed to admit that they had. The woman who told me that she had eaten from dumpsters did not admit to panhandling. One visitor to MSP, an alcoholic who was known to panhandle, was called a "disgrace to women" by another woman, with nodded agreement from several others. Apparently, the more a woman distances herself from the mainstream, as some street people do either by choice or by circumstance, the more alien they become to the majority of the homeless women who view themselves as temporary visitors to shelters. Although panhandling by men in the streets has a long tradition in American society, a woman approaching strangers and asking for money conveys an image that is repellant to most homeless women.

Another distinction between homeless men and homeless women is in socialization among the homeless. Several studies (Garrett & Bahr, 1973; Harper, 1982; Spradley, 1970) have shown that homeless men tend to be more group oriented, whether drinking together, setting up shanty towns or even traveling together. Homeless women, by contrast, tend to be the loners. Although more than half of the questionnaire group indicated that they had female friends and/or kept in touch with female relatives, these were usually women who were a part of their world before they became homeless. Many of the women in the emergency shelters will talk to one another, but they do not stay in the shelter long enough to become friends. It is only when they move to transitional shelters where they may stay for longer periods of time that the women begin to develop friendships with fellow residents such as Ann and Alisha, and Carol and Vivian, residents at Upton House who had become close to each other. Although the women at My Sister's Place sometimes chatted with each other, they rarely went together to Our Daily Bread to eat. They showed sharp distrust of other homeless women by asking volunteers to watch their belongings while they used the bathroom, went outside to smoke, or visited Our Daily Bread. One woman said, "They'll steal my things if I leave them here." This seems to be a distrust of strangers more than a distrust of women only.

The women often found themselves living in a "woman's world" in the various shelters. The women's shelters are run by women, and even the Salvation Army shelter, which will accept families with fathers, has a female director and is staffed primarily by women. The stereotype of women not being able to get along with women seems to be dispelled by the reactions of many of the women in this study. Over and over again they commented on the care and concern that they had received from these service providers. This does not mean that every woman responded this way, but the majority spoke in positive terms. Women in the mainstream maintain networks with other females. These networks may be in the form of female family members who manage social functions such as family dinners, birthdays, holiday celebrations, and other festive occasions. Another type of network is that of female friends who talk on the phone, eat lunch and shop together. Mainstream women also participate in groups such as Parent Teacher Associations, women's clubs, and sport groups, all of which may be predominantly female. Homeless women must leave such networks behind, for the most part. Although they may have contact with female friends and relatives, this is not on a regular basis. For this reason, many homeless women may turn to the female service providers for support. Female residents in transitional shelters often stop by the offices of service providers just to chat, as if to reassure themselves that there is someone who cares. If the shelter provider is an older woman, some residents may turn to her as almost a substitute mother, as in the case of Sister Marilyn at Marian House.

The homeless women in this study also felt a bond with other women, although it was not expressed in these terms. To explain why I needed their help, I said that I was writing a book on the needs of women who found themselves in shelters, and that I hoped this would help women in the future by improving conditions for the homeless. Almost without exception, women were willing to answer the questionnaire, and many agreed to be interviewed more extensively. The women often asked what the title of the book would be. When I told them *Silent Sisters,* there would frequently be a pause, and then a nod, and sometimes, "I like that," or "That's good." When I explained that this research would take time to gather and might be too late to help them, numerous women said that as long as it helped someone, that was what counted.

During the interviews, I always asked the women what advice they would give to other women that might help them avoid homelessness. Some of the answers were:

No matter who you are, stand up for what you believe. Don't take abuse from husbands. It will affect the children.

Always make sure that you have a reliable support system.

Go to work and have a job. Take care of your health—so you don't have to be out of work.

Look out for yourself. Listen to others, but beware of people who don't have your best interests.

Leave alcohol and drugs alone.

Educate yourself as much as possible. Because with all my troubles, that's one thing that they can't take away from me.

Don't depend on no man to give you nothin'. Nothin'!

My mother told me, "The only way you be in the gutter is because that's where you want to be at." And that's the truth.

These responses, based in many cases on bitter personal experience, reflect the values that the women had when I interviewed them. Ironically, the speakers were recommending that women be independent determiners of their own lives, the very qualities that they themselves have been unable to utilize.

Other women recommended religion as a support system. "Have faith in God and faith in yourself," said one. And from another, "Trust in Christ. No matter how far out in left field you go, He's going to be in your corner." The reliance on religion may have been a lifelong support system, or it may have developed since the woman became homeless. Several women, when asked what items they took with them when they became homeless, noted that the Bible was one of the five most important items that they took with them. In addition to seeking help from God, some of the women believed that the President could also make a difference. One woman seemed to speak for many homeless women when I asked her what she would say to the President if she could meet him. Her reply: "Women in displaced situations need all the help they can get. Anything he could do would be a blessing."

FEARS, HOPES, AND DREAMS

To continue to be homeless was the fear most often listed by the women staying in emergency shelters. It is surprising that more women did not list this, but this may be explained by the fact that they were in shelters when they answered the questionnaire. None of the women in transitional shelters listed this as their greatest fear, possibly because they were more optimistic or felt more secure in long-term housing. Their answers to the question "What is your greatest fear?" reflected other concerns. One of the fears that several expressed was a return to the condition that had precipitated their homelessness—for example, their alcoholism or drug addition. Because some of the women had been homeless before because of their dependency, they were keenly aware that they could begin to drink or take drugs again, and once more find themselves in the streets. For this reason, most of the women who were living in transitional shelters and had these problems were attending Narcotics Anonymous or Alcoholics Anonymous meetings several times a week. This was required by Marian House, but was optional at the houses sponsored by the Women's Housing Coalition. Nevertheless, some women do "go out," a term used by these organizations to mean a return to substance abuse. Lydia is an example of someone who has been in and out of AA for years.

For some women, their greatest fear may be the prospect of having to survive independently after leaving a transitional shelter. Alisha, who told everyone at Upton House that she was going to her sister's in West Virginia to be with her children, surprised everyone by moving back with the husband who had physically abused her. A few weeks after leaving the shelter she called Ann and explained that she had rejoined her husband because he "needed her." Alisha may not have been able to face the prospect of providing for herself and her three children and thus moved back with her husband. Another fear that the women expressed was emotional loss. Two women used almost identical words to describe their feelings:

> *Elizabeth B.: As soon as I get close to someone, they leave, screw you around, or die.*

> *Cookie: Somebody gets close and I lose them. My life has been like that—pure rejection.*

The women have lost so much: their homes, their possessions, sometimes their families, and even their children. The mothers who were without their children were concerned that they would lose custody permanently. They viewed the childrens' living arrangements as temporary and were, in some cases, planning to go to court if necessary to regain their children when the mothers' lives were more stable. For a woman who does not have permanent housing, nor the adequate income to provide it, this seems an impossible dream. Additionally, some of the women were deinstitutionalized, and regaining custody under these circumstances may be extremely difficult. When I asked her to describe her future, Elizabeth A., whose former husband had custody of their three children and had remarried, sweetly smiled and said, "I'll be in a nice place to live— maybe a little house and the kids will be back with me again and my husband will be back with us, too." Elizabeth A. had been hospitalized four times in the previous three years for mental illness. She may never regain custody of her children.

Still other women expressed a fear of males. One woman said that women wouldn't hurt people the way men do, referring to both physical and emotional pain. Another woman said that she was afraid that she would again choose a man who was wrong for her, and another said, "A man tried to kill me once. I've had a hard life." Previously abused wives were afraid that their husbands might find them. Four of the women had been physically abused as children by their fathers, and three women told me that they had been raped before they became homeless. In addition, one woman who had lived in the streets for several years told me that she was always afraid of being "slugged with a piece of wood by a man for money I don't have." One elderly lady had been mugged for an empty handbag. Another had her large tote bag snatched from her as she walked down the street. She was very upset because her Social Security papers and her medicine for high blood pressure were in the bag. It would require a lot of walking from DSS to the hospital clinic and hours, if not days, of her time to replace these two items. With experiences such as these, it is not surprising that a number of the women are afraid of men.

Still another fear that was expressed by only two of the women directly, but was inferred by many, focused on their identities as homeless women. One said, "I see myself as a street person and it scares me to death." Another stated that she was afraid of "being alone and sick and nobody to care." When I asked women to describe where they would be in five years, one replied, "If it's the same life I've been living, I don't want to live. You don't have a reason to live, it's no kind of life." Although this particular woman saw the future in bleak terms, the majority were much more optimistic.

In addition to their fears, the women were also asked to identify their greatest hopes. Half of the women included a home as their first priority, and several listed their children as their first priority. Only a small percent of the women expressed the need for a job as their future goal, while a few others commented that improving their own mental health was their first goal. One woman's first priority was for her husband to get a job and another woman wanted her "independence." The women who desired homes commented:

To have a home and to be happily settled with my kids.

A decent place to live.

I'll be in a nice place to live—maybe a little house and the kids will be back with me again.

I want to be married and secure in my own home.

To be in a nice house.

A place of my own.

To have a little house.

The woman who seemed to have the most elaborate version of her future explained:

I have hopes that I can reach the American dream: a little white house, a picket fence, the dog out in the backyard. I still want to be with a man. I hope that we're happy. I don't think it's a fantasy. I think it could work out. And I don't see anything wrong with having that dream.

The majority of women looked to a future where they would again have a home. How they would obtain their own places was often a question to which they had no answer. It is revealing that only a small number of women mentioned work as their first priority. The women who spoke of a home apparently did not see themselves as wage earners, or as people capable of financially providing for a home. Some women, in spite of their negative experiences as dependent females, cannot break free of dependency on a male breadwinner.

This is in sharp contrast to Bogue's (1963) study in which the hope that the men placed first was for a job, their second desire was for health, and their third was for money to escape skid row. The women, by contrast, wanted a home first, their children second, and their mental health third. These wishes reflect very different cultural values, for the men see work as the means to an end while the women see the end and do not identify the means. For some of the women interviewed, a man would provide the home, thus enabling the women to achieve the other two goals, although there was no man in their lives at the time of the interviews. Apparently for some women, the patriarchal family structure is desirable because a man will supposedly solve all of the problems.

A few women saw themselves as the determiners of their futures. The women who mentioned work first, such as a lab technician, a nurse's aid, and a counselor, mentioned independence as the result of their jobs. It is also informative that although 100% of the women have worked in the past, only three women saw themselves as active participants in their futures, while the remainder saw themselves as passive dependents in their dreams. Without such self-determination, the hope of permanently escaping homelessness seems merely wishful.

A WAY OUT

The way into homelessness for women is not a single, precipitous route, and the way back into the mainstream will vary from woman to woman. Although agencies may provide food and shelter, these alone are not the solutions to homelessness. Some women rejoin the mainstream; others remain in the cycle of moving from shelter to shelter, or move back with family or friends only to return to the shelters when problems resurface. Hanging onto their mainstream values, why do some women leave homelessness behind and how do shelters help the women to fulfill their dreams? Dot's account of her experiences and her return to the mainstream illustrate one success story.

A black, 38-year-old mother of a 23-year-old daughter, Dot became homeless because of drugs. She was born in Baltimore and quit school in the seventh grade when she became pregnant at 15. She did not marry the father of her child, and she and her daughter remained with Dot's mother. Dot said, "I could have worked, but I never tried." She lived with her mother and 11 brothers and sisters; her father had left her mother when Dot was two weeks old, but there were three step-fathers during the following years. She even had a step-grandfather about whom she commented, "We always had step—we never had our own." Her mother was "bitter about the people she lost."

From the time she was 15, Dot had been involved with men. For years, she used "reefers," but eventually she moved on to heroin that was provided by her boyfriend who had to shoot her up because she didn't know how to use the needle. After several years, she quit heroin, but began to use cocaine. By this time she was "hanging out on Pennsylvania Avenue" in Baltimore and was picked up for prostitution. She was sent to Lutheran Hospital because she was ill, and she eventually found her way to Marian House. Although she left Marian House for a month and went back to her old friends and her drug habit, she finally returned to Marian House and her life began to change for the better. The structure, care, and concern that the staff provided were the support system that Dot credited with helping her get her life together.

After eight months, Dot moved to Upton House where she lived for ten months. At Upton House she had more freedom and could test her new independence while knowing that there was a support system available. During this period she got a job as a laundress in a downtown nursing home, and on weekends worked at Marian House as a night supervisor. Dot explained what has made the difference for her:

I've had a lot of men who took good care of me. They didn't teach me to do things on my own, but they were good to me. I'm getting older. But I want to grow older the right way. Not because of drugs, or men I've slept with. I realize I've short-changed myself. If society is willing to help, I'm willing to help society. [What has caused the change in you?] I made a promise when I came out of drugs. If I ever see anybody who is mentally distraught, if I can help them, I will do my best. Sometimes you see someone drowning, you can't help them. But I try. Someone told me about being sexually abused. I know a lot of people like that. Someone can say, "This is the reason I feel so much pain." The girls I work with, I have learned about my hurts and myself. They've had the pain I've had. So people confide in me. They tell me their troubles. "Dot knows," they say.

[How have the shelters helped you?]

Marian House was the beginning. This [Upton House] is the middle. The third step is my own place. I'll take Marian House and Upton House to the next step. Now I know how to save money. I learned that at Marian House. The women here have helped. The overall pain—all of us have been through a dramatic stage that has brought us here. To find out if we are growing or regressing. We all grow here—some few haven't, but it wasn't their turn to grow. We need a structure to fall back on. Some of the women are going to go back to the same way of life because the hurts and problems that brought you to this place, it's not going to change. It could even happen to me. But I have met more people in these 18 months who are about help, that you can't help but become a caring person yourself. All the good things in life are God working in you.

A month after I interviewed Dot, she was financially able to move into her own apartment with the help of a Section 8 and the income from her jobs at the nursing home and at Marian House. I met her several months later at Marian House where her introduction of me to the residents was responsible for the many women who volunteered to be interviewed. Dot said, "We are all women, and we have to help each other. By giving a few hours of your time, you might make a difference. We have all been there. We know." The one thing that she did not mention was that she was a role model to the women at Marian House of one who had made it back. Dot is now a permanent member of the staff at Marian House and was appointed to the Mayor's Task Force on planning a family shelter for the homeless in Baltimore City.

Ann is another former resident of Upton House who has moved into her own apartment. She tried to get one of the other residents at the shelter to share an apartment, but that did not work out. After losing one place because of the other women's indecision, Ann, with the help of the housing outreach counselor for WHC, found a Section 8 apartment that she could afford on her SSI check. She was able to obtain used furniture, and the outreach counselor worked closely with Ann for the next six months to ensure that she got the support she needed. Two years later, Ann still lives independently in her apartment and has made a transition to the mainstream.

Carol, the 33-year-old widow, secured a position at a retail store where she worked for six months before moving on to a larger retail chain and into her own apartment. When I took her home one night several weeks after she had moved in, she had a bed, a chest of drawers, a kitchen table, and two chairs. The living room was empty. A stove and refrigerator were already in the apartment. Carol's pride in her home was evident as she took me through each small room and told me how she planned to decorate. She is presently a buyer for the retail chain, has bought a car, and serves on the board of the Women's Housing Coalition.

The women from Marian House and Upton House who have moved into their own residences and are functioning in the mainstream were all women who took some responsibility for themselves. Ann, Carol, and Dot were all night managers at Upton House at different times, a responsibility that enabled them to prove to themselves that they were capable people. In addition, both Dot and Carol obtained jobs that also reinforced their self-images and provided them with incomes. Ann's break from her controlling and managing family gave her the time she needed to prove to herself that she could live independently. The women themselves had to take action, but the Women's Housing Coalition provides an atmosphere in which women who are able are given the time to heal from the initial trauma of homelessness and to grow to the point where they are ready to live on their own. For some, this may mean a job that will allow the woman to be self-sufficient, as with Dot and Carol. For others, it may mean a lifetime on SSI or even welfare and subsidized housing, but with careful management of their incomes, these women need not rejoin the ranks of homelessness again if they can find subsidized housing.

Other women do not move into apartments, but instead move into efficiency rooms such as the ones at Basilica Place, a residence for the elderly operated by Catholic Charities. Whatever housing they find, they will be faced with living alone, and although this is the desire that so many of them expressed, to have a home of their own, once it appears to be a reality, there may be some concern at leaving the company of the women in the shelters behind and having to prove that one can make it on one's own. Vanessa, the former prostitute who had completed her nursing certification and had a job at a hospital in the city, was spending her last month at Marian House looking for a place to live. She expressed fear at the idea of living on her own for the first time in several years when she said, "Marian House provides support. I don't know if I can make it out there."

For the women who are suffering from severe mental illness, the way out of homelessness is more complicated. In addition to the problem of little or no money, they are still plagued by the illnesses that were responsible for their homelessness. Some of these women are incapable of functioning on their own and need communal living arrangements. Only Project Plase and the Park Avenue Lodge offer such services. Many of the women need daily medication in order to function, as well as needing supervision and assistance in handling the little money they have. For these women to rejoin the mainstream is a step that most are incapable of making alone. The Park Avenue Lodge attempts to prepare these former street women to rejoin the mainstream, but it may be that the major service this shelter provides is preventing these women from returning to the streets where they will eventually become too ill to survive. The Park Avenue Lodge has offered a secure, clean, and safe environment administered by caring people.

Because slightly more than half of the women in the questionnaire group indicated that they were in a shelter for the first time, where do they go when they leave the emergency shelters? Apparently, they either return to their families, move in with friends, or rent a room until they begin the cycle again.

If these women are to leave homelessness behind them permanently, more than food and shelter are needed. Job training and counseling are essential for many of the women who are able to work if they are to become financially independent. All of the women in the interview group and 86% of the questionnaire group had worked outside their homes. These are impressive figures that on the surface would indicate that this is a group that could easily rejoin the work force. Yet further questioning revealed that many had work experiences of a year or less at a job, and that the majority of these jobs had been in low-paying service jobs. A 40-hour week's pay at the minimum hourly wage ($3.80) does not allow anyone to live independently. The women need training in areas that will allow them to earn a decent wage.

In addition to job training, the women need a support system that will be there if they need help. Marian House allows a woman eight months of job and personal counseling, education in the form of GED classes, and training in financial planning so that at the end of her stay, a woman is able to rent a room or apartment. The Women's Housing Coalition offers follow-up support for six months after a resident leaves. Women who are recovering from homelessness may be as fragile as women who are recovering from an illness or alcoholism or drug addiction. They need time and a support system to act as a safety net until they have proven they can survive alone. It requires determination and action for a homeless woman to rejoin the mainstream. It also takes patience. Section 8's, the major financial help in obtaining housing, are very scarce, and one may wait months before obtaining one. The wait for an apartment in a project may take two to five years.

Dot, Carol, and Ann are homeless women who have successfully rejoined the mainstream. Although both Marian House and the Women's Housing Coalition keep annual figures on the number of women who move on to independent living, there is little follow-up over an extended period of time. Occasionally a former resident will call the director and inform her of what is happening, but the initiative lies with the former resident. One shelter provider reasoned, "Most of the women, once they are independent, want to put this chapter of their lives behind them. They don't want to maintain contact with us." Apparently, once they have returned to the mainstream, they try not to look back.

7

A MATTER OF GENDER

The primary purpose of this research was to determine if there is a subculture of female homelessness, particularly for Baltimore women. Secondary purposes were to compare the lives of homeless men to those of homeless women; to analyze the effects of gender difference for homeless women; and to assess the impact of stereotyping the homeless. My interviews with both the homeless and their service providers also gave me the opportunity to comment on changes and improvements for helping the homeless.

CULTURES OF HOMELESS MEN AND HOMELESS WOMEN

The research of Bogue (1963), Bahr (1973), Spradley (1979), and others have established that a subculture of homeless men exists. Exhibiting distinctive behaviors, learning the jargon of tramping, and assimilating tramp values enables a man to become a member of this subculture of American society and to leave the mainstream behind. To what extent have homeless women developed such distinctive patterns of behavior and/or distinctive systems of shared knowledge? Is there a subculture of homeless women and if so, how does it compare to that of homeless men? The similarities between the two subcultures are scant. Both may have come from very poor economic backgrounds that precipitate their fall down the economic ladder into homelessness. Both may rely on social agencies for food, shelter, clothing, and income. Both may frequent the same sections of the city because this is primarily where the services are offered. It is my conclu-

sion, however, that, for numerous reasons, female homelessness does not constitute the distinctive subculture of male homelessness.

Although homeless men and women both prize shelter as equal only to food
in the struggle for survival, these two groups have different attitudes toward
shelter. Bahr (1973) found that fewer than 10% of the men in his study slept in
missions. Like some women, many men resist missions because of the religious
thrust of the charity. However, men also avoid missions because their use implies a lack of survival skills that are prized in their group. By contrast, the
majority of homeless women in Baltimore wanted shelter that was safe and
clean, and no one in this study turned down shelter because it might reflect a
lack of independence, nor did I ever hear a woman criticize other women for
accepting shelter. When I asked, "How do you feel about women who sleep in
the streets and won't go to shelters?" one response was, "Women shouldn't
have no [sic] business being out on the streets. It's okay for a man." Another
respondent said, "A woman don't know how to defend herself. Any woman
who chooses to stay out in the streets is crazy." The women believed that the
safety and comfort of shelters took priority for survival.

Language reflects attitudes as well as values. Spradley (1970) found nearly
100 categories of sleeping places or "flops" used by the tramps in his study. No
woman in this study ever used the term "flop" or any other slang term that
designated a sleeping place. The women used only the specific name of a
shelter—The YWCA, the Mission, the Salvation Army.

David Kaplan and Robert A. Manners (1972) have stated that "investigat-
ing the language in cultural domains will lead into the cognitive categories used
by the members of a society in ordering and thinking about these domains" (p.
147). A special use of language is one of the features that characterizes tramp
culture that has an elaborate argot with special terms for sleeping places, kinds
of tramps, and even kinds of time. Homeless women also have a domain of
words that is used by them more frequently than by the general public but these
are not of their creation (See Appendix 7). For example, the alphabet soup of
government programs that are available to the homeless such as SSI, AFDC,
GPA, and Section 8's are unfamiliar to the majority of people in the mainstream
unless they have had occasion to use such programs. Homeless women learn
these terms and what they stand for because they are told about DSS by either
service providers or by other homeless women. Although some women refer to
Karis Hospice as "the mission" and some refer to any detoxification unit as
"the detox," the major distinction between the use of words by homeless
women and that of homeless men is that the women have not coined their own
words.

Unlike tramp culture, which has an extensive and unique jargon, the homeless women of Baltimore have no words that they have invented. The women
who were involved in this study did not use any words that represented a
language unique to their condition. They have learned the vocabulary of wel-

fare and the names and addresses of shelters and soup kitchens. If a woman did not understand what "DSS" was, someone might explain that this stood for the Department of Social Services. If a woman did not know what Our Daily Bread was, she was informed of the soup kitchen's location and its hours. The shortening of place names occurred occasionally, but no invented words were used. The police were called the police or the cops, and the doctors and nurses at Springfield State Hospital were referred to by those professional terms. The homeless women of Baltimore have learned the geography of the city as it relates to homelessness, and they use the names of various service providers such as the YWCA or My Sister's Place in place of street names, but this does not constitute the language of a subculture.

In addition to language differences, another major difference between the tramp and the homeless female is attention to appearance. The homeless male is less particular about his appearance and more concerned with warmth and comfort. Most homeless women, on the other hand, make every effort to present a "normal" or "attractive" and mainstream female appearance. In part this is a strategy—in this way they can mingle and blend in with middle-class shoppers and tourists without attracting attention to themselves.

One of the most popular donations to any woman's shelter is clothing. The women at Upton House got very excited when anyone brought clothing that was in good condition. They tried to coordinate colors and styles to create attractive outfits. Women at the Salvation Army and My Sister's Place, where choices were often more limited because of the larger number of women being served, also tried to select stylish items that fit them. For most women, clothing reflects a contact with mainstream culture. For example, most women bathed and took pride in their appearance, using makeup and attempting to maintain attractive hair styles. By contrast, many tramps are not clean-shaven or cleanly dressed.

The possessions that homeless men and women consider valuable also reveal differences. Men tend to travel light, carrying items they consider necessary for survival. By contrast, the women tend to value items that either provide identity, such as marriage licenses or photographs, or security, such as a pillow or a souvenir, all reminders of a safer and more settled time. One might say that women tend to be more sentimental, while men seem more practical when they select the possessions that they will carry with them into homelessness. Yet the women's items that provide strong ties to the past are also reminders of the mainstream, and may seem to function as threads to keep the women from permanently separating themselves from society.

One of the behaviors associated with tramp culture has been the mobility of the men as they have moved around the country looking for work. Bahr (1973), in his research on skid-row men, however, found that between 40–60% of the men were natives of the city or region in which they were homeless. The women have exhibited similar patterns: approximately half of both groups were natives to Maryland. Approximately 15% have come from within a 300-mile radius of Baltimore. This would seem to indicate that unlike the tramps of the early decades of this century, the majority of homeless men and women of today are not taking to the highways. Additionally, approximately 70% of the women reported that they had spent the last year in Maryland. This also substantiates the view that they are nonmigratory.

Women have also been less prone to move around the city on their daily errands. Once located in a shelter, a woman has tended to think of her immediate surroundings as her neighborhood. Her geographic world has been determined by the location of the services she uses such as DSS, medical facilities, and stores. Although the men in Bogue's (1963) research lived in skid-row sections of cities, the Baltimore women were not restricted to a particular area of the city and could have moved about if they had chosen to do so. It has been their lack of bus fare and perhaps their fear and timidity or even unfamiliarity with other parts of the city that have caused the women to remain, for the most part, within walking distance of their shelters.

Homeless men and women also differ in the area of employment. Bogue's (1963) research on skid-row men revealed that 86% of the men in his study had worked in the year before becoming homeless. By contrast, the women in Baltimore revealed a much smaller percentage of workers (approximately 30%) during 1986-87, the year they answered the questionnaire.

Two thirds of all of the women had worked during the last five years and about half (50%) had worked during the last two years. Of the women who had worked, however, the majority had worked at jobs such as sales clerk, waitress, cashier or factory work, all of which require little or no training or specific skills. The wide discrepancy between Bogue's figures and those of this study may be accounted for by several factors. During the year previous to becoming homeless a number of these women were mothers who stayed home with children, women in mental hospitals, and women still living at home with a spouse. Approximately 41% had never worked longer than a year at one job.

One of the major differences between the results of Crystal's (1984) study and this study is employment. Crystal found that women were three times more likely than men to have never been employed. The results of my study show that 100% of the women interviewed had been employed at some time in their lives, and that 87% of the women in the questionnaire group had been employed. These women were not the welfare mothers that the stereotype portrays. Yet only 9% in the interviewee group reported loss of job as causing their homelessness, and only 13.5% of the questionnaire group stated this as the cause. It seems obvious that although most homeless men have been wage-earners over long periods of their lives, homeless women worked only sporadically and had not been the principal breadwinners before becoming homeless.

Using Spradley's (1970) definition of a culture, "a set of rules they employ, the characteristic ways in which they categorize, code, and define their own experiences," (p. 7) as a yardstick, the homeless women of Baltimore have not established a separate culture of homelessness, although there are distinctive patterns that characterize the way most of the homeless women have operated.

Based on these patterns, it is my conclusion that the world of female homelessness is in such an embryonic stage that it barely constitutes a subculture of American society. The women, however, have acquired distinctive knowledge about homelessness. They have learned about different kinds of shelters and the services they provide. They know about soup kitchens, their hours, and types of food served. They have learned the geography of the city and the locations of agencies that can provide them with services.

In addition, women living in either emergency or transitional shelters have adapted to the multitude of rules and regulations set forth by service providers. The interfusion of women into surviving as the homeless who utilize services available to them is not a lengthy process, but can be "learned" in a short period of time. Several women told me that no one taught them anything about being homeless. They found shelters listed in the yellow pages of the phone book or went to Our Daily Bread where someone sent them to a shelter. Often they were sent to shelters when they were released from hospitals or prisons. Homeless women have usually helped a woman who did not know where to go for the basic necessities, but this could have been learned relatively quickly on one's own. For the street women who do not come into contact with agencies, there may be a more extensive initiation, although a woman who works with street people stated that the "bag ladies" travel alone because they are so alienated from everyone.

The characteristic ways in which homeless women "categorize, code and define their own experiences" (Spradley, 1970, p. 7) are still those of mainstream America. These women have not changed their general values or beliefs. They were encouraged to believe in middle-class values even though many of them have come from very poor backgrounds. In the mainstream, a man traditionally is the principal breadwinner and a woman is a wife and mother who belongs in the home. Repeatedly the women shared the same dream of being in a home again with the children. If they were homeless when I interviewed them, that is not where they saw themselves in the future.

These mainstream values have even affected their views of themselves. They often fear that they are lesser people than they thought and have labeled themselves as failures. This perception was repeated by numerous women. However, this does not indicate a change in the standards they were using, but reflected the way they rated themselves on the standards they brought with them from the mainstream. Without their connections to others, they had judged themselves as failures as women. Their greatest anxiety was that homelessness might become a permanent way of life for them and that this disconnectedness might become permanent as well.

Although many of the women have lost the daily contact with family and friends that they had before they were displaced, many of them have tried to keep in contact with females who were once part of their lives. For example, half of the women had regular contact with a female relative, and half had regular contact with a female friend.

Like several other researchers, Bahr (1973), in his study of skid-row males, found that the homeless man has disaffiliated himself from family, friends, and mainstream society with little thought for the past or the future. This was not true of homeless women in this study. Not only did many of them have regular contact with a female relative or friend, but also they tried to maintain contact with their children. Affiliation and concern for their children was their principal interest. This seems to indicate that although the women have been physically separated from their former female networks, many of them have continued some contact.

Another reason for the lack of a subculture of homeless women is that women have not had time to develop the domains that are characteristic of a culture. It has only been ten years since the first numbers of women began appearing at shelters in Baltimore. The culture of the tramp developed over a span of more than 100 years. Tramps were also highly mobile and large numbers of them traveled throughout the country spreading the culture. In contrast, the majority of the Baltimore women had spent 1987 in Maryland. Additionally, although the numbers of homeless women are increasing annually, as is the total number of homeless (Alvarez, 1990), there are not tens of thousands of them in Baltimore. Instead, they are in small groups scattered throughout the downtown area.

In 1988, women constituted approximately 20% of the homeless in the United States (Ropers, 1988). Their individual efforts have gone toward surviving in order to regain the mainstream rather than in forming a cohesive and distinctive group outside society. The basic commonality they share is not language, dress, or behavior, but gender. Being female impacts on homelessness in a variety of ways.

One of these is the dependency on men that many of these women exhibited prior to becoming homeless. The majority of the women had not been encouraged to choose work that would make them financially independent. Instead, they had been conditioned to see themselves as wives and mothers. This dependency on the man as a means of support left the woman bereft of financial and, often, emotional resources when the boyfriend or husband left.

In addition to their male dependence, many homeless women, for example, Alisha and Lisa, had chosen partners who were physically abusive. Other women, like Vanessa and Elizabeth, grew up in homes in which their fathers or step-fathers had sexually abused them. These kinds of relationships are so psychologically destructive that it is no wonder these women have had difficulty living in the mainstream. By the time they are homeless and living in shelters, their self-esteem has been so ravaged that they are fearful of making any decisions. I have seen women in emergency shelters who seemed trance-like or "shell-shocked." They were so emotionally drained by the experience of losing their men that they were apathetic.

Although single homeless women with children were not the main focus of this study, these mothers were frequently in the group of women who were staying in emergency shelters and who completed the questionnaire. In recent years, single mothers have been the fastest growing segment of the homeless population (Rubin, 1988). Support payments from the fathers of their children are often non-existent and the mothers are dependent on aid such as AFDC. This also makes gender a contributory factor in female homelessness, for homeless men do not take their children with them. The "welfare mother" has become a stereotype in the American class system. In the last decade this stereotype has also become homeless. In addition to facing the uncertainties of finding food and shelter, the homeless mother is responsible for the survival of two human beings. A woman who can no longer provide food and shelter for her child may give her child to relatives or to foster care. The stigma of losing custody may prevent a woman from regaining custody of her child even if she has rejoined the mainstream because she has failed previously to provide for her child. A mother who gives up custody may be regarded as a questionable risk for the future.

POLICY IMPLICATIONS

Suggestions for Agencies and Services

The ethnographic study of a group cannot only provide information on the subject group, but it can also provide suggestions for agencies that have contact with that particular group. The media, the government, and service providers impact on the lives of homeless women and are therefore a part of the world of homelessness. Mainstream attitudes toward the homeless influence these agencies and can range from sympathy and concern to hostility and avoidance. The attitudes of the public and the media reports on these attitudes wax and wane. Homelessness has become a national as well as a local media event. Confined to articles in the winter months in the past, homelessness now attracts attention year round. The emphasis has changed as well. Reporters previously attempted to focus on individuals in human interest stories or "tragic" stories such as a "bag lady" freezing to death in the streets or a fast by the late Mitch Snyder (Smith, 1987; "2000 Rally For Affordable Housing at U.S. Capitol," 1988). More recently, however, the news articles have focused on new approaches to providing services for homeless people, such as the use of a former army barracks at Fort Meade, Maryland, to house women and children, ("Barracks," 1987) and James Rouse's Enterprise Foundation formed in 1982 to provide affordable housing for low-income people, including the homeless (Gunts, 1990). These changes seem to reflect shifts in attitudes and government policies as well. The passage of the appropriation of $327 million by the Senate to partially fund the Urgent Relief for the Homeless Act, which was authorized by the Senate in April 1987, also helped emphasize the critical need for services for the homeless ("Homeless Win Senate Battle," 1987). In Maryland, the Governor's Advisory Board on Homelessness produced the bulletin *Homelessness: Recommendations for State Actions* (1986), which contains nine objectives ranging from the prevention of homelessness to provisions for permanent housing. These and similar efforts are to be applauded.

Advocates for the homeless have been heard in some cases. Help for the homeless, however, should include the views of the homeless themselves. They have experienced homelessness firsthand, a situation that is different from all others. They are analogous to people who have gone through divorce, rape, or other life experiences that differ from those of the majority. For these reasons, it is necessary to understand the cultural dimensions of the situations of both the women and the helping agencies. Service providers do listen to the women and they are aware of many of the problems of homeless women. They often represent the women in policy issues at local and state levels. Service providers, however, often view the homeless from their own cultural backgrounds and this may prevent them from understanding the needs of the clients they serve. The lives of homeless women are controlled and regulated to a great degree by the agencies that provide them with services. Yet these controls are imposed from the top with little or no direct input from homeless women. The residents of emergency and transitional shelters have specific ideas and suggestions for what they need.

Service providers are to be commended for their labors and, in many instances, exemplary service to the homeless. Working long hours with women who are often ill, withdrawn, helpless, and confused requires patience, compassion, and deep concern for the human condition. There are no luxuries for the homeless, nor for those who work with them. The shelters and soup kitchens are restricted to the bare necessities. The salaries of the service providers are notoriously low, for they are often working for charitable and nonprofit organizations. One shelter director reported earning $12,500 a year (personal communication, 1986). A shelter provider told me that the burnout rate is very high for service providers, and that is substantiated by the fact that six of the seven women who were key individuals in the shelters involved in this study are no longer working with the homeless. In spite of these problems, the shelters remain open. New people who are interested in the homeless are recruited. The staff at the Park Avenue Lodge, for example, has a very caring attitude and a calmness when dealing with emergencies. They give each resident individual attention, whether it is simply talking about the day's activities or administering the medication needed to function outside of an institution. In the first year of operation, the director was hoping that funds would be available to keep the shelter open all year. As one resident told me: "In a year all I do is go from shelter to shelter. What's that for a year? But thank God for this shelter or I'd be on the streets." Catholic Charities has continued to meet the need and the Park Avenue Lodge now serves 13 women.

Marian House, which originally provided shelter for former jail inmates but also accepts other homeless women, has a high success rate in helping women rejoin the mainstream. In fiscal year 1988–89, one half of the women served were able to leave and live on their own (Marian House Annual Report, 1989). The Women's Housing Coalition also provides an atmosphere in which a woman need not be pressured by time constraints. She may take a year or more to recover from the trauma of homelessness, find a job or apartment, and move into independence. The Women's Housing Coalition provides women with a secure setting and a staff that recognizes that homeless women need recreation and fun as much as other people do. I always heard laughter when I visited Upton House.

The Salvation Army, the largest emergency shelter for women in Baltimore, fights burst water pipes, overcrowding during blizzards, lead paint problems, and a reliance on volunteers to provide a bed and three meals a day to countless homeless people. Faced with numerous children clamoring through the building and accepting all types of homeless women, the staff remains calm and caring. Their canteen is the only contact that some of the homeless have with a helping agency, and the staff at the shelter does everything it can to see that the truck runs, even if the director has to pay for the gas with her own credit card.

Job Training

There are, however, areas that need improvement. For example, service providers are beginning to understand the need for helping with more than food and shelter. Financial independence is paramount if the women are to succeed in the mainstream. One area that needs to be addressed by service providers is job training programs for shelter residents. Although a substantial percentage of the women had worked during the last five years, the jobs were in unskilled, low-paying service work. Many of the working women had become homeless within a matter of as little as a month or within several months, indicating that there were no additional financial resources to help them when they become unemployed.

Financial Planning

Another area that needs redress is teaching the women the skills of planning their monthly budgets. To address the financial problems that these women have experienced in the past, the staffs at some transitional shelters are helping women budget and handle their money, even if it is only a monthly GPA check. Marian House requires residents to place one third of any income into individual saving accounts so that a woman will not only learn how to save, but will also have a security deposit and the first month's rent at the end of her eight-month stay at the shelter. More transitional shelters need to conduct workshops for homeless women on how to handle their money.

Self Esteem

Another problem for homeless women is their low self esteem because they have "failed" as wives and mothers. Several aspects of the shelters need to be changed to make them less dehumanizing and more welcoming to improve the self-images of the residents.

One of these changes would be to use the names of the residents when addressing them. In some of the shelters the women seem to have become mere faces and are seldom addressed by name. Our names are our identity more than anything we possess. Not to use a name reduces the person to the status of a thing or a non-person. The humiliation of not having a home and the consequent loss of identity is overwhelming enough without being a nonentity to the people who are supposed to help. This may seem an unreasonable request. After all, shelter providers often deal with new homeless women every day and to require them to learn the names of individual residents in a shelter as large as the Salvation Army, which may have 30 adult residents at a time, may seem overwhelming. Yet to simply talk to the women without using their names ignores their individual identities. The majority of shelter providers do try to use the women's names.

An additional factor that would help to make the shelters less threatening and alien would be the use of curtains and pictures in the shelters. My Sister's Place has managed to use pictures drawn by the children and donated artwork to brighten the walls of its daytime shelter. The YWCA shelter allows for privacy because each woman has her own room. This is appreciated by the residents, but the stark furniture, lack of curtains, and bare walls give the appearance of a rented room, not a home. These amenities could be provided by volunteers. For women who have carried pillows and stuffed ducks as well as kitchen plaques with them, these small touches would provide a sense of home, a feeling of tangible security. The searching of shopping bags and handbags at some shelters also reduces the women to the level of suspicious persons and such procedures ignore the dignity of any woman, regardless of her circumstances. We all require respect from others in order to have self-respect. There are good reasons why shelter providers do not want alcohol or drugs in the shelters because some of the women have abused both. But to operate on the premise that a person is innocent until proven guilty is not only a basic tenet of American society, but also humane. All shelters have rules that if a person becomes disorderly, she must leave. This effectively removes the offender without insulting the innocent majority.

There are other ways in which to develop independence and self-respect in the women. Throughout the months of interviewing, I was struck by the defeatedness of so many of the women, especially those in the emergency shelters. Their answers to questions seemed to indicate that they were not in control of their lives, and in several ways that is true of anyone using shelters and soup kitchens. As a homeless woman for even a few days, my overwhelming impression was that I had abrogated my freedom of choice: my food; my place to sleep; my time to shower, sleep, and eat; when I would go indoors for the night; even my clothes, had I chosen to accept clothing from one of the shelters would have been determined by others, not by me.

The words that come to mind to describe these conditions are child-like dependency or institutional care. Either condition is demeaning to an adult. Although soup kitchens are straining to meet the financial burden of feeding so many, is there not some way that a cafeteria style service could be provided and the guests be allowed to choose between two main dishes? Can't an emergency shelter allow guests to enter over a period of several hours before closing the doors for the night? Involving the women in even such small choices can encourage them to believe that they are in control of some portion of their lives. The regimentation of the women's lives while they are residents encourages dependence, not independence. If a woman is not allowed to even determine at what time she will take a shower, how can she be asked to find an apartment or job, or to handle a salary or welfare check economically? The women who have been alcohol-, drug-, or male-dependent need special help in regaining control of their lives and in viewing themselves as the active determiners of their lives rather than as passive victims. Group sessions with volunteer psychologists or social workers (if money is not available to fund such services) would help these women take a giant step toward returning to and remaining in the mainstream.

The women clearly demonstrated that they are not the disaffiliated people that many have believed them to be and that they want to return to the mainstream. The vast majority have a link with either a female relative, a female friend, or their children. The shelter providers working with mothers of children under 18 told me that being reunited with their children was one of the primary motivators for women working toward goals that would bring them back into the mainstream. Shelter providers can use these affiliations to help women by allowing the residents to have female relatives and friends visit them, and by providing shelter space for mothers who could then bring their children for an overnight visit. Only a few emergency shelters have facilities for mothers and children. In Baltimore, a long-term transitional shelter for mothers and children was opened in 1987, but more are needed (Evans, 1987). Because single women with children are acknowledged by service providers to be the largest growing segment of the homeless, it is imperative that this serious need be addressed. A very young mother with a three-week-old baby allowed me to hold her baby while she filled out a questionnaire. Shy and withdrawn, she did not want to be interviewed, and when she finished the questionnaire, she took her baby in her arms, looked at me, said, "I don't know where we are going from here."

One of the complaints by several women about the Salvation Army shelter was that single women and women with children are living on the same floors. The director of the shelter makes every effort to keep the two groups separated, but when the shelter becomes crowded, this is not always possible. In 1990, the Salvation Army applied for a permit to expand its shelter with a large addition in the rear of the existing shelter. This met with vehement opposition from neighborhood residents, who objected to more homeless moving into the area. The City Council eventually gave its approval.

The shelter providers in Baltimore have become aware of different groups within the population of homeless women, and this is reflected in the various shelters that serve specific groups such as the Park Avenue Lodge for former street women, and the House of Ruth for battered women. The Park Avenue Lodge has space for only 13 women. This shelter cannot begin to address the needs of the many deinstitutionalized and mentally ill women in Baltimore. All levels of government must assume financial responsibility for providing the half-way houses that were an integral part of the Community Mental Health Act of 1963 (Alter & Stille, 1984). A newspaper article concerning a new program inviting lawyers to volunteer their services on behalf of the homeless suggested that "Former patients in state hospitals may have to fight to get promised out-patient care" ("New program," 1987, July 9, p. F2). The private sector is exhausting its resources (Canzian, 1990), and the state of Maryland has allocated only $2.8 million in fiscal year 1990 for the needs of all homeless in the state (Speakers' Bureau, 1990).

There are still women whose specific needs are not being met, however. Although the WHC opened a single-room occupancy hotel for single women in the fall of 1990, there is still a need for shelters for women aged 18 to 21, and for alcohol and drug-dependent women. When women from these various groups are mixed indiscriminately, only the basic needs of food and shelter can be met and the individual attention that is necessary to help these women rejoin the mainstream must be sacrificed.

Transitional shelters are attempting to help women rejoin the mainstream, and have succeeded in helping numerous women find apartments and jobs. These women, however, are still in need of a support system for at least a year after they leave a shelter. Because of the pressing needs of the women remaining in the shelters, once a woman leaves, she is more or less expected to be independent. The Women's Housing Coalition uses its housing outreach counselor to not only locate housing, but also to keep in touch with a woman and to help her with any problems she may have for a period of six months in order that she may remain in the community. Other transitional shelters need to offer similar services. Women who move into their own residences could be encouraged to return to their former transitional shelters once a month or more to visit with their previous house friends and share their successes and problems with women who may soon follow them. This would not only provide a support network for the mainstreamer, but might also help motivate residents of the shelter. This networking might not appeal to all women, for the director of one shelter told me, some women want to put the entire experience of homelessness behind them, and they refuse to acknowledge that they were ever in that situation (Carole Melvin, personal communication, Oct. 10, 1989). Because of the helpfulness I found most homeless women willing to give me in my research, I believe that many women would respond positively to such a program.

Such volunteers from among the previously homeless might also serve in an outreach program, for there needs to be a greater effort by service providers in informing those on the streets of shelter availability. Granted that shelters are often overwhelmed with the number of homeless, especially in inclement weather, there is still a critical need to communicate to the homeless who do not come in. Two women (of the 122 who participated in this research) told me that they did not know about My Sister's Place or the shelters. One spent several days and the other several weeks in the streets before learning of a shelter. At Jacob's Well, for example, is an organization that sends workers into areas where the homeless congregate in an attempt to inform them of the available services. Using the media to disseminate information is not the answer, because the homeless rarely have access to television sets or newspapers. Outreach workers could help save lives.

Although the private sector is straining to meet the financial needs of providing for the homeless, there are areas in which volunteers could benefit the homeless and themselves. A carpet salesman in Baltimore who is a graduate of Cooper Union Art School spent four months in 1986, and again in 1990, giving art lessons to the residents of the houses sponsored by the Women's Housing Coalition. The Women's Housing Coalition paid for the supplies, and the artist met with the seven to nine women who attended the bimonthly sessions. Their interest and delight in producing pencil sketches and colored pen drawings of various still lifes were exceeded only by their pleasure in seeing their work displayed at the annual WHC board meeting held in December 1986. On another occasion, the residents were provided the opportunity to spend two days in a condominium in Ocean City, Maryland, provided by an anonymous friend. The women were thrilled at the chance to swim in the ocean and have a vacation. Several women also told me that they would like to go to museums if there were volunteers to drive them. Shelter providers should be aware that the women need such experiences almost as much as they need food and shelter.

One group that would benefit from volunteering to work with the homeless is the police. A 20-minute session in the squad room on a cold night is insufficient to explain the problems of homelessness or how to deal with homeless people. Spending several hours a month when off duty working in a shelter or on the Salvation Army canteen, as did an Anne Arundel County fireman one night a week, would sensitize the police to the needs and humanity of street people. An alternative would be to invite someone who works with the homeless to speak to the force when they are in the police academy and have the opportunity to visit shelters. It is necessary for the police to recognize that these are human beings with special needs and to treat them accordingly.

Perhaps the greatest need in the area of homelessness, and the most difficult to accomplish, is to change the attitude of many in the mainstream toward the poor and the homeless. The homeless women have been members of the mainstream. They are not the "bag ladies" of the stereotype. They are not hopeless, for many with the proper help can and have rejoined the mainstream. They are not undeserving, for the majority are struggling to leave homelessness behind them. They are not parasites, for most have worked in the last five years and many can and will work again. Even descriptions of homeless women often used by service agencies are misleading. They are too broad and there are cross-overs; for example, a substance abuser who becomes mentally ill and who may be evicted when her boyfriend leaves. The causes of homelessness may be as many as the number of homeless people. Although such classifications are convenient, they tend to reinforce the mainstream stereotype.

As long as the "welfare" mother who has nine illegitimate children by nine different fathers, and the "bag lady" who has large amounts of money in her shopping bags but likes living in the streets remain as stereotypes, women will continue to receive only enough for subsistence living. Public assistance will remain as unpleasant as possible as long as the poor are viewed as responsible for their own plight because they are too lazy to get jobs. The very country that can raise millions for aid to Africa can also allow the sprinkling of chlorine bleach on garbage in dumpsters, the abandonment of the homeless in deserts without food or water, and the razing of urban campsites used by the homeless. Each of these outrageous acts was reported in the media, and yet no national outcry was heard (Salerno et al. 1984; Hope & Young, 1986; Leo, 1985). As a nation we deplore the abuse of human rights by the governments of other countries; as a nation we ignore our own shameful treatment of our most impoverished citizens. The women I interviewed have not expressed their views in the state legislature or the Congress. The President did not hear Yvonne's plea to "stop the missiles and start feeding the people." Only when we recognize their individuality and grant them the human dignity they deserve will we begin to hear the voices of our sisters.

REFERENCES

Actors, pols join sleep-in. (1987, April). *Safety Network,* p. 3.

Allsop, K. (1967). *Hard travellin'.* London: Hodder and Stoughton.

Alter, J., & Stille, A. (1984, January 2) Homeless in America. *Newsweek,* pp. 20–29.

Auletta, K. (1982). *The underclass.* New York: Random House.

Alvarez, R. (1990, November 29). Ranks of homeless swelling in Maryland. *The* (Baltimore) *Sun,* pp. B1, B4.

Bahr, H. M. (1973). *Skid row.* Oxford: Oxford University Press.

Bahr, H. M., & Garrett, G. R. (1976). *Women alone: Disaffiliation among urban women.* Boston: Lexington Books.

Barracks at Fort Meade transformed into shelter. (1987, June 10). *The* (Baltimore) *Sun,* p. B2.

Bassuk, E. L. (1986, February). A psychiatrist to the poor tells the toll of the uprooted life on families and the friendless. *People,* pp. 86–88.

Bassuk, E. L., Rubin L., & Lauriat A. (1984). Is homelessness a mental health problem? *American Journal of Psychiatry, 141,* 1546–1550.

Baxter, E., & Hopper, K. (1981). *Private lives/Public spaces: Homeless adults on the streets of New York City.* New York: Community Service Society.

Birch, E. L., (Ed.). (1985). *The unsheltered woman.* Rutgers, NJ: Center for Urban Policy Research.

Blumberg, L. U., Shipley, Jr., T. E., & Barsky, S. F. (1978). *Liquor and poverty.* New Brunswick, NJ: Rutgers Center of Alcohol Studies.

Blumenthal, W. H. (1952). *Women camp followers of the American revolution.* Philadelphia: George S. MacManus.

Bogue, D. J. (1963). *Skid rows in American cities.* Chicago: Community of Family Study Center, University of Chicago.

Box-Car Bertha. (1937/1975). *Sister of the road.* New York: Harper & Row.

Breakey, W. R., & Fischer, P. J. (1985). Down and out in the land of plenty. *Johns Hopkins Magazine,* pp. 16–24.

Burnham, L. (1986). Has poverty been feminized in black America? In R. L. Lefkowitz & A. Withorn (Eds.), *For crying out loud* (pp. 69–83). New York: Pilgrim Press.

Canzian, E. (1990, December 2). Resources strained in Baltimore area. *The* (Baltimore) *Sun,* pp. A1, A11.

Chisolm, E. (1987, January 1). A new year. *The* (Baltimore) *Sun,* pp. D1, D7.

Corcoran, M., Duncan, G. J., & Hill, M. S. (1984) The economic fortunes of women and children. *Signs, 10,* 232–248.

Crockett, S. (1988, January 10). Help for the homeless is growing. *The* (Baltimore) *Sun,* pp. B1, B2.

Crouse, J. M. (1986). *The homeless transient in the Great Depression: New York State. 1929-1941.* New York: State University of New York Press.

Crystal, S. (1984). Homeless men and homeless women: The gender gap. *Urban and Social Change Review, 17,* 2–6.

Cuomo, M. M. (1983). *1933/1983—Never again.* Report to National Governor's Association Task Force on the Homeless. Portland, ME.

Dolgoff, R., & Feldstein, D. (1980). *Understanding social welfare.* New York: Harper and Row.

Ehrenreich, B. (1986). What makes women poor? In R. Lefkowitz & A. Withorn (Eds.), *For crying out loud* (pp. 18–28). New York: Pilgrim Press.

Evans, M. C. (1987, November 24). Renovated school will shelter homeless families. *The* (Baltimore) *Sun,* p. C3.

Flynn, R. (1986, March). Surviving the streets: Seven days with Baltimore's homeless. *Baltimore Magazine,* pp. 62, 132–136.

Flynt, J. (1972). *Tramping with tramps.* Montclair, NJ: Patterson Smith.

Frece, J. W. (1986, December 26). At soup kitchen, turkey and dry socks. *The* (Baltimore) *Sun,* pp. E1, E6.

Garrett, G. R., & Bahr, H. M. (1973). Women on skid row. *Quarterly Journal of Studies on Alcohol, 34,* 1228–1243.

Garrett, G. R., & Bahr, H. M. (1976). The family background of skid row women. *Signs, 2,* 369–381.

Gilligan, C. (1982). *In a different voice.* Cambridge, MA: Harvard University Press.

Gimlin, H. (Ed.). (1982). *Editorial research reports: The homeless: Growing national problem.* Washington, DC: Congressional Quarterly.

Glaude, S. (1986). Female-headed families and chronically unemployed adults. *Ending poverty.* Conference conducted by Consumers Union, Washington, DC.

Golden, S. (1986). Daddy's good girls. In R. Lefkowitz & A. Withorn (Eds.), *For crying out loud* (pp. 233–247). New York: Pilgrim Press.

Governor's Advisory Board on the Shelter, Nutrition, and Service Program for Homeless Persons. (1986). *Homelessness: Recommendations for State Action.*

Greater Baltimore Shelter Nework. (1986). *Annual Survey of Shelter Providers in Central Maryland.* Baltimore, MD: Author.

Greene, D. I. (1986, November 27). A few of city's homeless find warmth, friendship by tracks under expressway. *The* (Baltimore) *Sun,* pp. C1, C8.

Gunts, E. (1990, March 6). James Rouse appeals for low-cost housing. *The* (Baltimore) *Sun,* pp. E1, E5.

Hagen, J. L. (1986, May). *Gender and homelessness.* Paper presented at the 1986 National Association of Social Workers National Conference on Women's Issues, Atlanta, GA.

Harper, D. A. (1982). *Good company.* Chicago: University of Chicago Press.

Heiss, J. (1986). Family roles and behavior. In F. A. Boudreau, R. S. Senott, & M. Wilson (Eds.), *Sex roles and social patterns* (pp. 89–102). New York: Praeger.

Homeless win senate battle. (1987, July). *Safety Network, p. 1.*

Hope, M., & Young, J. (1986). From back wards to back alleys: Deinstitutionalization and the homeless. *Urban and Social Change Review, 17,* 7–11.

Hopper, K., Baxter, E., Cox, S., & Klein, L. (1982). *One year later: The homeless poor in New York City, 1982* New York: Community Service Society.

Hopper, K., & Hamberg, J. (1984). *The making of America's homeless: From skid row to new poor. 1945-1984.* New York: Community Service Society of New York.

Housing now! The birth of a major housing movement. (1989, November). *Safety Network,* p. 1.

Irelan, L. M. (Ed.). (1968). *Low-income life styles.* Washington, DC: U.S. Dept. of Health, Education, and Welfare.

Kamerman, S. B. (1986). Women, children and policy. In B. C. Gelpi, N. C. M. Hartsock, C. C. Novak, & M. H. Strober (Eds.), *Women and poverty* (pp. 41–63). Chicago: University of Chicago Press.

Kaplan, D., & Manners, R. A. (1972). *Culture theory.* Englewood Cliffs, NJ: Prentice Hall.

Karp, A. (1986, December 10). Message service sells "bag lady grams" but some aren't buying. *The* (Baltimore) *Sun,* pp. B1, B3.

Kennedy, W. (1983). *Ironnweed.* New York: Viking.

Lefkowitz, R., & Withorn, A. (1986). *For crying out loud.* New York: Pilgrim Press.

Leo, J. (1985, March 11). Harassing the homeless. *Time,* p. 68.

LeVine, R. A. (1984). Properties of culture. In R. A. Schweder & R. A. LeVine (Eds.), *Culture theory* (pp. 67–86). New York: Cambridge University Press.

Marian House. (1989). *Annual report.* Baltimore, MD: Author.

Maryland Department of Human Resources. (1986, August). *Where do you go from nowhere: Homelessness in Maryland.* Baltimore, MD: Author.

McCord, J. (1986, November 10). Soup kitchen picks holiday for its last meal. *The* (Baltimore) *Sun,* pp. C1, C9.

McKinney Act reauthorized and expanded. (1990, November). *Safety Network,* p. 1.

Millions form human chain to aid hungry. (1986, May 26). *The* (Baltimore) *Sun,* p. 1.

Mitch Snyder is alive. (1990, August). *Safety Network,* p. 1.

Monkkonen, E. H., (Ed.). (1984). *Walking to work: Tramps in America, 1790-1935.* Lincoln, NE: University of Nebraska Press.

Murray, H. (1986). Time in the streets. In J. Erickson & C. Wilhelm (Eds.), *Housing the homeless* (pp. 53–69). Rutgers, NJ: Center for Urban Policy Research.

National Coalition for the Homeless. (1986). *National neglect/National shame. America's homeless: Outlook, winter '86-87.* Washington, DC: Author.

New program is seeking volunteers to provide legal help for homeless. (1987, July 9). *The* (Baltimore) *Sun,* p. F2.

Ollove, M. (1986, February 23). Homeless man's life a tale of shelters, soup kitchens. *The* (Baltimore) *Sun,* p. 1.

Pearce, D. (1978). The feminization of poverty: Women, work, and welfare. *Urban and Social Change Review, 11,* 28–36.

Ringenbach, P. T. (1973). *Tramps and reformers 1873-1916.* Westport, CT: Greenwood Press.

Ropers, R. H. (1988). *The invisible homeless.* New York: Human Sciences Press.

Rossi, P. H. (1989). *Down and out in America.* Chicago: University of Chicago Press.

Rousseau, A. M. (1981). *Shopping bag ladies: Homeless women speak about their lives.* New York: Pilgrim Press.

Rubin, N. (1988, November). America's new homeless. *McCall's,* pp. 118–123.

Salerno, D., Hopper, K., & Baxter, E. (1984). *Hardship in the heartland.* New York: Community Service Society of New York.

Schneider, J. C. (1986). Skid row as an urban neighborhood, 1880-1960. In

J. Erickson & C. Wilhelm (Eds.), *Housing the homeless* (pp. 167–189). Rutgers, NJ: Center for Urban Policy Research.

Schur, E. M. (1983). *Labeling women deviant.* Philadelphia: Temple University Press.

Siegal, H. A. (1974). *Outposts of the forgotten.* Unpublished doctoral dissertation, Yale University, New Haven, CT.

Singer, M. (1968). Culture. In D. L. Sills (Eds.), *International encyclopedia of the social sciences.* New York: MacMillan and Free Press.

Smith, J. A. (1987, January 28). 25 hold chilly candlelight vigil in honor of homeless woman who died outdoors. *The* (Baltimore) *Sun,* p. G1.

Snow, D., Baker, S. G., & Anderson, L. (1986). The myth of pervasive mental illness among the homeless. *Social Problems, 33,* 407–423.

Speakers' Bureau. (Producers). (1990). Slide/Tape presentation. Baltimore, MD: Action for the Homeless.

Spradley, J. P. (1970). *You owe yourself a drunk.* Boston: Little, Brown.

Spradley, J. P. (1979). *The ethnographic interview.* New York: Holt, Rinehart & Winston.

Spradley, J. P., & McCurdy, D. W. (1980). *Anthropology: The critical perspective.* New York: John Wiley and Sons.

Statistical abstract of the United States. (1989). Washington, DC: U.S. Department of Commerce, Bureau of the Census.

Statistical abstract of the United States. (1990). Washington, DC: U.S. Department of Commerce, Bureau of the Census.

Stengel, R. (1986, November 24). Down and out and dispossessed. *Time,* pp. 27–28.

2000 rally for affordable housing at U.S. Capitol. (1988, December). *Safety Network,* p. 1.

U.S. Congress. Senate Committee on Appropriations. (1983). *Street people.* (98th Cong., 1st sess. S. Hrg. 98–57.) Washington, DC: U.S. Government Printing Office.

Wallace, S. E. (1965). *Skid row as a way of life.* New York: Harper.

Wallis, C. (1989, December 4). Onward, women! *Time,* pp. 80–89.

Weiner, L. (1984). Sisters of the road. In E. H. Monkkonen (Ed.), *Walking to work: Tramps in America 1790-1985* (pp. 171–188). Lincoln, NE: University of Nebraska Press.

Welfare Advocates. (1990). *Guide to Welfare.* Baltimore, MD: Author.

Wilson, M. (1986). Deviance and social control. In F. A. Bordreau, R. S. Senott, & M. Wilson (Eds.), *Sex roles and social patterns* (pp. 294–302). New York: Praeger.

Wolins, M., & Wozner, Y. (1977). Deinstitutionalization and the benevolent asylum. *Social Service Review, 51,* 604–621.

Young, L. (1986, December 14). Feeding the hungry. *The* (Baltimore) *Sun,* pp. G1, G6.

APPENDICES

APPENDIX 1: QUESTIONNAIRE

1. How old are you?
   - [ ] 18–30
   - [ ] 31–50
   - [ ] 51–80

2. Which of the following describes your present status?
   - [ ] single
   - [ ] married
   - [ ] separated
   - [ ] divorced
   - [ ] widowed

3. Do you have any children?
   - [ ] yes
   - [ ] no

4. If you have children, how old are they?
   - [ ] 1 month–5 years
   - [ ] 6–12 years
   - [ ] 13–18 years
   - [ ] over 18 years

5. If you have children under 18, where are they?
   [ ] with father
   [ ] with your relatives
   [ ] with father's relatives
   [ ] in foster home
   [ ] with me
   [ ] don't know
   [ ] given up for adoption

6. Which of the following are you?
   [ ] Black   [ ] Jewish
   [ ] Greek   [ ] American Indian
   [ ] Hispanic   [ ] Polish
   [ ] Oriental   [ ] Italian
   [ ] White

7. In what state have you lived for the longest period during the last year? _____

8. In what state were you born? _____

9. Until you were 18 or left home, with which of the following did you live the longest? How long?
   [ ] both parents in same house _____
   [ ] mother alone _____
   [ ] father alone _____
   [ ] mother and stepfather _____
   [ ] father and stepmother _____
   [ ] grandparent _____
   [ ] relative _____

10. Have you ever worked outside your home?
    [ ] yes
    [ ] no

11. If so, what jobs have you held?

    _____
    _____
    _____

    How old were you when you first worked? _____
    What is the month and year of your last job _____

12. What is the longest period of time that you worked at the same place?
    [ ] less than 6 months
    [ ] 6 months–1 year
    [ ] 1–3 years

[ ] 4–10 years
[ ] more than 10 years

13. What is your highest level of education?
    [ ] less than grade 8
    [ ] grades 9–12
    [ ] high school graduate
    [ ] 1–2 years of college
    [ ] college graduate
    [ ] master's degree
    [ ] technical school

14. Do you have a female relative you have regular contact with? If so, who is she?
    [ ] yes _____
    [ ] no

15. Do you have a female friend with whom you have regular contact?
    [ ] yes
    [ ] no

16. How many different times have you stayed at a shelter this year?
    [ ] one time
    [ ] 2–5 different times
    [ ] 6 or more different times

17. How many times have you stayed at a shelter during the last 5 years?
    [ ] one time
    [ ] 2–5 times
    [ ] 6 or more times

18. Which of the following was the cause of your homelessness?
    [ ] loss of job
    [ ] eviction
    [ ] illness
    [ ] domestic problems (husband or boyfriend)
    [ ] domestic problems (other family members)
    [ ] emergency (fire)

19. At what age did you become homeless? _____

20. How long have you been homeless?
    [ ] less than 6 months
    [ ] 6 months–1 year
    [ ] 1–2 years
    [ ] more than 2 years

21. List the 5 things that you considered most important for you to keep or take with you when you became homeless.

    _____

    _____

    _____

    _____

    _____

22. What is your greatest fear?

    _____

23. What is your greatest hope?

    _____

24. If you have a religion, which of the following is it?
    [ ] Protestant   [ ] Greek Orthodox
    [ ] Catholic   [ ] Oriental
    [ ] Jewish   [ ] Other
    [ ] Moslem

25. Have you ever been in jail?
    [ ] yes
    [ ] no

26. Have you ever been hospitalized for a mental illness?
    [ ] yes
    [ ] no

27. Have you ever lived in the streets?
    [ ] yes
    [ ] no
    If so would you be willing to discuss it with me? _____

28. At this very moment what do you need most?

    _____

    _____

    _____

29. Where are you presently staying?
    [ ] Salvation Army
    [ ] YWCA
    [ ] Project Plase
    [ ] Karis Hospice
    [ ] Woman's Housing Coalition
    [ ] Antioch House
    [ ] House of Ruth
    [ ] Other _____

APPENDIX 2: QUESTIONNAIRE RESPONSES

Question number	Response	Questionnaire		Interviewees	
		Frequency (100)	Percentage (100)	Frequency (22)	Percentage (100)
1.	18–30	59	59.0	8	36.4
	31–50	33	33.0	13	59.1
	50–80	8	8.0	1	4.5
2.	single	54	54.0	11	50.0
	married	20	20.0	1	4.5
	separated	12	12.0	4	18.2
	divorced	12	12.0	5	22.7
	widowed	2	2.0	1	4.5
3.	yes	67	67.0	10	45.5
	no	32	32.0	12	54.5
4.	1 month–5 years	40	40.0	5	22.7
	6–12 years	23	23.0	3	13.6
	13–18 years	11	11.0	2	9.1
	over 18 years	9	9.0	4	18.2
5.	with father	7	7.0	4	18.2
	with your relatives	8	8.0	2	9.1
	with father's relatives	4	4.0	0	0.0
	in foster home	11	11.0	1	4.5
	with me	26	26.0	0	0.0
	don't know	0	0.0	1	4.5
	given up for adoption	0	0.0	1	4.5
6.	Black	60	60.0	10	45.5
	Greek	0	0.0	0	0.0
	Hispanic	3	3.0	0	0.0
	Oriental	0	0.0	0	0.0
	White	28	28.0	10	45.5
	Jewish	3	3.0	1	4.5
	American Indian	4	4.0	1	4.5
	Polish	1	1.0	0	0.0
	Italian	2	2.0	0	0.0
9.	both parents in same house	34	34.0	10	45.5
	mother alone	25	25.0	8	36.4
	father alone	2	2.0	0	0.0
	mother and stepfather	10	10.0	1	4.5
	father and stepmother	2	2.0	0	0.0
	grandparent	10	10.0	1	4.5
	relative	13	13.0	1	4.5
10.	yes	87	87.0	22	100.0
	no	13	13.0	0	0.0
12.	less than 6 months	15	15.0	2	9.1
	6 months–1 year	24	24.0	8	36.4
	1–3 years	29	29.0	6	27.3
	4–10 years	15	15.0	4	18.2
	more than 10 years	5	5.0	1	4.5

(*Continued on next page*)

APPENDIX 2 (*Continued*)

Question number	Response	Questionnaire		Interviewees	
		Frequency (100)	Percentage (100)	Frequency (22)	Percentage (100)
13.	less than grade 8	4	4.0	2	9.1
	grades 9–12	38	38.0	3	13.6
	high school graduate	31	31.0	10	45.5
	1–2 years of college	20	20.0	2	9.1
	college graduate	7	7.0	3	13.6
	master's degree	0	0.0	1	4.5
	technical school	2	2.0	0	0.0
14.	yes	58	58.0	12	54.5
	no	42	42.0	7	31.8
15.	yes	53	53.0	16	72.7
	no	44	44.0	3	13.6
16.	one time	73	73.0	13	59.1
	2–5 different times	22	22.0	7	31.8
	6 or more times	5	5.0	1	4.5
17.	one time	64	64.0	13	59.1
	2–5 times	25	25.0	6	27.3
	6 or more times	7	7.0	2	9.1
18.	loss of job	13	13.0	2	9.1
	eviction	15	15.0	1	4.5
	illness	16	16.0	10	45.5
	domestic problems (male)	23	23.0	5	22.7
	domestic problems (family)	26	26.0	3	13.6
	emergency	9	9.0	1	4.5
20.	less than 6 months	75	75.0	7	31.8
	6 months–1 year	11	11.0	8	36.4
	1–2 years	6	6.0	1	4.5
	more than 2 years	5	5.0	5	22.7
24.	Protestant	26	26.0	13	59.1
	Catholic	19	19.0	2	9.1
	Jewish	1	1.0	0	0.0
	Moslem	3	3.0	0	0.0
	Greek Orthodox	0	0.0	0	0.0
	Oriental	0	0.0	0	0.0
	Other	37	37.0	3	13.6
25.	yes	20	20.0	11	50.0
	no	78	78.0	8	36.4
26.	yes	22	22.0	9	40.9
	no	76	76.0	11	50.0
27.	yes	28	28.0	9	40.9
	no	70	70.0	11	50.0
29.	Salvation Army	90	90.0	3	13.6
	YWCA	0	0.0	0	0.0
	Project Plase	0	0.0	0	0.0
	Karis Hospice	0	0.0	0	0.0
	Woman's Housing Coalition	3	3.0	10	45.5

APPENDIX 2 (*Continued*)

Question number	Response	Questionnaire		Interviewees	
		Frequency (100)	Percentage (100)	Frequency (22)	Percentage (100)
	Antioch House	0	0.0	0	0.0
	House of Ruth	0	0.0	0	0.0
	Marion House	6	6.0	9	40.9

Note: Questions 7, 8, 11, 19, 21, 22, 23, and 28 required individualized responses that are not listed here.

APPENDIX 3: GUIDELINES FOR GUESTS OF KARIS HOSPICE

Therefore, if any man (or woman) be in Christ, he (or she) is a new creation; old things are passed away; behold, all things are become new.

2 Cor. 5:17

Welcome!! We the staff sincerely believe that all who enter our doors come by God's providential leading in their lives, not by "chance" or "bad luck." We believe all come for a purpose greater than shelter, food, and clothing. What is that "greater" purpose? To hear about the love, grace, and mercy of God revealed to all through His Son, Jesus Christ. We pray that you come willing to receive what is shared about Jesus Christ as well as our other services.

Karis Hospice is a temporary shelter. It is not a hotel; therefore, do not treat it as such. Everything we offer to you is absolutely free. Please make yourself comfortable. Please do *not* make yourself at home.

The following guidelines were developed to insure that your stay here is comfortable and safe. You are required to follow all of them while staying here.

Bible Studies and Services

Attendance at all Bible Studies and Services is mandatory. You will be told in advance when they are scheduled. Evening prayer meetings are optional; however, all are welcome to attend.

Possessions

The staff reserves the right to inspect all containers brought into the Hospice.

All medication must be turned in to the office to be dispensed according to directions at specified times.

You must take all of your personal belongings with you when you leave. The Mission cannot be responsible for anything you leave here.

APPENDIX 4: ELEANOR D. CORNER HOUSE
FIFTH FLOOR SHELTER HOUSE RULES

Length of Stay

Residents can stay up to a maximum of 8 weeks if they sign a Service Plan. Otherwise a resident will be asked to leave after 3 days.

Curfew

Residents are asked to be in the building by 12:00 midnight weekdays and weekends.

Meals

Meals will be served in the third-floor dining room. It is important to get to meals on time as it will not be possible to have a meal if you miss a given mealtime. Breakfast, 7 to 7:30; Lunch, 12 to 1; Dinner, 5 to 6.

Housekeeping

Residents are required to make their beds by 9 a.m. and to keep their rooms clean. Please clean the bathroom after you use it. Each resident will be assigned a general housekeeping task each day. Task assignment and rotation will be worked out with the staff.

Laundry

Each resident will be responsible for washing her own clothing. Details for use of the washing machine and dryer will be worked out with the staff. Residents are asked to check with the staff person before using the machine.

Food

No food will be allowed in the rooms. No cooking allowed anywhere except in the kitchen.

APPENDIX 5: WHC OVERVIEW
OF INTAKE PROCEDURES

Referrals to the Women's Housing Coalition come via telephone from area shelters, hospitals, and the Department of Social Services. A potential resident is interviewed by the Service Director at Upton House. She is given a tour of the house and an overview of the program including rules, procedures, and services. We attempt, at the initial interview, to evaluate her independent-living skills and her ability to function in a community environment. When possible, she is assisted in transporting her belongings to her new, temporary home.

Upon her arrival, an intake form is completed. She would also sign a form stating that her first two weeks are probationary. After two weeks she is asked to sign a residential contract enabling her to stay for up to six months. If she wishes to move on before her time is up, she is encouraged to do so. After six months her contract will be reviewed by the Service Director who determines if she would benefit from an extension.

While in the program, she meets regularly with the Service Director and Housing Counselor to identify and implement her goals and to build on her strengths. Residents with a history of psychiatric problems are encouraged to seek outpatient counseling and to comply with medication schedules.

It is our hope that, by providing safe, affordable housing in a supportive environment, a woman may move through her immediate crisis into a more stable living situation.

APPENDIX 6: RULES AND PROCEDURES FOR MARIAN HOUSE

Orientation

On the day of arrival each new resident will receive an initial orientation to the program after which she will sign a copy of the rules and a contract.

During her first two weeks in the residence, each woman will be considered in orientation. With her counselors, she will plan her first two weeks' activities to include medical exam, securing of the medicaid card, and appointments with appropriate agencies. For the first week, her curfew hours will be 6:00 p.m. She must remain in Marian House the first weekend.

As part of the first day's orientation, the new resident will meet with the Night Supervisor to discuss household procedures.

Each resident receiving an income will give a deposit of $10.00 toward the room key, blanket, and linens provided to her by the program. At her departure, the $10.00 will be refunded if the key is returned, the blanket and linens are returned laundered, and the room is completely cleaned.

Finances

Each resident receiving an income of any kind must work out an individual budget plan with her counselor to include allotments for room/board, savings, and weekly allowance. Room and board will be figured on a sliding scale.

Upon securing employment, the resident will be charged an appropriate amount for the weeks when she was unable to pay room and board.

APPENDIX 7: DOMAINS

Food

WIC
Our Daily Bread
Urban Services
Franciscan Society
Grace and Hope Mission

Shelter

Section 8
The Y
Eve House
Trailways
Greyhound
The Hospice (The Mission)
Antioch House
Night Shelter (Park Ave.)
Project Plase
Upton House
Salvation Army
Lombard House

Income

SSI (Supplemental Security Income)
Social Services
A-90
GPA (General Public Assistance)
Food Stamps
AFDC (Aid to Families with Dependent Children)

Training Programs

Good Will
New Directions
Bradley Center

Parks

Charles Center

Clothes

St. Ignatius
My Sister's Place
Upton House

Hospital/Treatment

Carter Center
The DeTox (A detoxification unit)
Constant Care